Spotlight Poets

EXPRESSIVE MINDS

Edited by

Chris Walton & Steve Twelvetree

First published in Great Britain in 1998 by
SPOTLIGHT POETS
1-2 Wainman Road, Woodston,
Peterborough, PE2 7BU
Telephone (01733) 230749
Fax (01733) 230751

SB ISBN 1 84077 021 X

FOREWORD

As a nation of poetry writers and lovers, many of us are still surprisingly reluctant to go out and actually buy the books we cherish so much. Often when searching out the work of newer and less known authors it becomes a near impossible mission to track down the sort of books you require. In an effort to break away from the endless clutter of seemingly unrelated poems from authors we know nothing or little about; Spotlight Poets has opened up a doorway to something quite special.

Expressive Minds is a collection of poems to be cherished forever; featuring the work of twelve captivating poets each with a selection of their very best work. Placing that alongside their own personal profile gives a complete feel for the way each author works, allowing for a clearer idea of the true feelings and reasoning behind the poems.

The poems and poets have been chosen and presented in a complementary anthology that offers a variety of ideals and ideas, capable of moving the heart, mind and soul of the reader.

Chris Walton & Steve Twelvetree

CONTENTS

SHEILA DURBIN

I first tried to write a poem when I was seven and I feel sure that it was inspired by the strong rhythms of poems which had been read to me. I worked for some years as a teacher of French and later as a librarian, so language and communication have been a central concern in my professional life. My chief sources of inspiration are the natural world and my Christian faith. Often I find myself using material objects or situations to symbolise spiritual reality. I spent my first ten years in Ceylon (now Sri Lanka) and visited it again for a few months as an adult. Although it is a strikingly beautiful island it does not possess the variety of weather or the range of light and shade to be found in the UK. Perhaps that is my reason for attempting to suggest this range and variety in my poems.

Of recent years, one of my main themes has been the ways in which one's view of the world and experience of life change as one grows older - and also the ways in which they remain the same.

My hobbies have been reading, gardening and walking; unfortunately gardening is now much curtailed by arthritis, but I can still walk comfortably, which is a great blessing. Writing poetry is a source of great pleasure, and is something one can do as well, if not better, in later life; and that is a gift to be prized.

AND AS I EVER OLDER GREW, TIME FLEW

Old people in their rest-home sit quiet through the hours;
The embers of their vital flame, which once was strong as ours,
Are seldom stirred to brightness and dwindle day by day,
And little is the import of all they do and say.

We visit, offering chocolates and bringing scraps of news
From the great, bustling, noisy world beyond their sheltered views;
With little jokes and messages we rouse them from their dream,
And think, with fear and pity, how tedious days must seem.

But what with sleep and memories, perhaps it is not so:
Out-distancing the rest of us, for whom time still goes slow,
They, having passed through grief and joy, completing ages seven,
Are held within the hand of God, nearing the gate of heaven.

OCTOBER

How warm and golden the October sun,
Bright on the flowers and leaves that must decay!
Soon, soon the autumn's glory will be gone;
With leaf-fall, gold and scarlet stripped away.

The richness of the earth no more we'll see
But only winter's white, austere delights;
Black silhouettes of trees on paling skies
And distant stars that burn through freezing nights.

Prospects too often veiled in muffling mist;
For days or weeks grey clouds oppress the mind;
Hedgerows and fallen leaves are brown or dun,
Last, tattered remnants in the sighing wind.

Yet still the robin sounds a note of cheer
For, at midwinter, Christ's birth crowns the year.

AUTUMN MORNING

Such a dawn of change and surprise!
Sunshine, rain, grey clouds, blue skies;
A kaleidoscope of colour and light;
Trees of autumn a dear delight.

The year's first seagulls next I saw,
Flying inland, leaving the shore;
Circling, white against grey skies,
To lift the heart and draw the eyes.

They come from the pathless ocean, curled
Like a mantle of mystery, round the world;
Symbol and pledge of infinity;
That time shall lead to eternity.

WEATHER OF THE SOUL

A day of heavy showers and sun -
Winter still but April weather.
I looked and saw a radiant scene;
A bare tree clothed in flowing light,
With sunlit raindrops swayed by wind,
More strangely bright than summer trees
That boast white bloom or tender leaves.
God, who redoubles beauty's spell
By sending sunshine after rain,
Extends such bounty to our souls.
We, who repentance know, and grief,
Are dazzled as we stand and gaze,
After our tears, at love's bright blaze.

EAST OF THE SUN AND WEST OF THE MOON

Long ago in a Northern land
A tale was invented and told;
A tale with a luminous title,
Key to dream-cities of gold.
The story was soon forgotten,
But the title's remembered still:
It shines like a jewel in my mind,
Able to conjure at will
A mystic land full of marvels,
Where dragons and unicorns roam,
Where the lamb can lie down with the lion,
And every heart is at home.

One night the moon was rising
In a soft, translucent haze;
I turned to the other horizon,
Still flushed with the sun's last rays.
I was shaken with joy and wonder;
How strange, how strange to find
That I stood in the marvellous kingdom
That long had possessed my mind.
And we all may know, in the moonlight,
Or greeting the sun's bright face,
That we stand in the marvellous kingdom;
The kingdom of immanent grace.

WINTER MORNING

Who can regard the sun?
Its all-revealing rays
Dazzle the eyes of those
Who too directly gaze,
Yet on one misty morn
When moisture charged the air,
The sun, a soft red ball,
Muted, its glittering glare,
Rose in the winter dawn.

So if we seek God's face,
We cannot see it plain;
Its radiant holiness
Half-hidden must remain
Through sheer excess of light,
Yet, on a winter's morn,
God came to you and me -
Our God in human form -
For all the world to see.

THROUGH A GLASS, DARKLY

An autumn morning; sun on frosty grass;
My windowpane was blurred where heat met cold,
But yet a little space was clear - I saw
A rooftop and a patch of dawn-streaked sky;
Etched on that sky, an oak-tree spread its boughs,
Balanced and rounded as a peacock's tail.
I think - this life is like the misted pane;
A tiny peephole on infinity,
Till one day we shall see it perfectly.

THE SURPRISE

I never did like starlings!
With feathers dusty black,
With awkward, jerky strut,
Beauty and grace they lack.

One lucky day in April,
With showers come and gone,
I saw a budding may tree,
A wide lawn drenched with sun.

A flock of birds was feeding,
Black, shot with flecks of green,
Brilliant, fabulous,
And amethyst their sheen.

Surely they weren't starlings;
So bright an apparition,
With iridescent feathers,
That quite absorbed my vision?

Thus, when the light of heaven
Transforms our dingy hues,
We shall express the glory
That every life imbues.

THE DREAMER

How brightly pebbles shine in stream or pool,
A child's delight,
Yet taken from the water, lose their gleam,
Like a dream's flight.
The fearless diver rises from the deep,
Pearls in his hands,
And so the dreamer, bringing gold, returns
From unknown lands.
But, like fool's gold, this treasure will not stay,
Is marked for loss;
Evades the questing mind or is revealed
As merest dross.
Yet, on some lucky, unforgetting morn,
Safe in his hands,
He brings the treasure that will never fade,
From distant lands.

WALKING IN SPRING

I ventured out between the flying showers,
Whipped by the wind that shook the blossoms down,
And rain soon caught me - the cold rain of spring.
But great was my reward; fugitive gleams
Of sun soon strengthened; verdant trees and flowers
Flashed into vivid colour at its touch.
The clouds, blue-grey and washed with violet dye,
Echoed the hue of opening lilac bloom;
Against that foil of cloud a screen of trees,
Stirred by the wind, displayed their silver leaves,
Boldly illumined by the April sun.

SUMMER ENDING

Summer seemed endless; days of heavy heat
And glaring light; pale flowers and withered grass.
The forecast's only message - hot and dry;
The same again as far as we can see.
The country seemed becalmed, and all too like
That ancient ship, idle on painted seas.
Yet autumn had advanced; as the globe turned,
Time, that had seemed suspended, still moved on.
The rain came, and the stealthy change was seen;
Dull leaves were silvered, and the morning sun
Shone on bright berries, dewdrops on the grass.
Then came a new sound. Looking up, I saw
The wild geese flying.

The wild geese in a swift, advancing wedge,
Leaving our shores to seek a warmer land,
Before the great gales of the equinox.
The sound of their migration makes me dream
Of ultimate journeys, starry odysseys:
Distant worlds calling.

DAYBREAK

How often have I watched the strengthening light,
Black night grow pale, and colour newly born -
Blue of the sky, evergreen trees and shrubs,
Pink, gold and orange of the winter dawn;
These and all other hues since time begun,
Flung from the white-hot furnace of the sun.

MIDWINTER

Night wanes and brings a moment of illusion,
As I look out and see the bright reflection
Showing my warm, secure and lighted bedroom;
Yet just beyond there looms a shadowy landscape,
And now my door becomes strangely transparent,
As through it I discern trees, sky and rooftops,
Vague and remote, without detail or colour,
But every time I look my room grows fainter;
Bright patches I can see - a vase, a blanket;
My picture floats off the wall to hang in the sky,
Suspended in air, imprinted on grey cloud,
As the light strengthens and day dawns at last.
Soon I shall see my lighted room no longer,
But the vaster world in which I must adventure,
Leaving the lamplight, entering the sunlight.

CHANGES AND CHANCES

After an ill-starred day of bleak distress,
I woke, mistrusting what the next should bring.
The sky was grey, with weeping clouds, and wind
Stirred in the trees and chased the clouds along,
Till sun broke through with transient shafts of light
Which grew and strengthened, while the sombre clouds,
In tattered ranks fled fast across the blue -
The blue emerging sky which shone between;
Symbol of hope amidst life's changing scene;
Hope, the undying light along our way.

THE PRECURSOR

What shall I do when the ominous precursor,
With silent steps, comes knocking at my door;
The little sign that warns of pain or weakness;
That I can walk with confidence no more?

What else but watch the dawn or sunset colours,
And watch the wind that sweeps the clouds along,
And cherish beauty in each passing moment
More than I did when I was young and strong.

What else but think of those who've gone before me,
Whose fortitude and courage light the way,
Who after joys and travails of their journey
Have reached the realm of everlasting day.

What else but turn to friends who are still beside me
To help me bear the burden and the fear,
Who through the years have shared in joy and sorrow,
But in these latter days are yet more dear.

And then I'll speak to God who waits to hear me,
Confessing all my helplessness and woe,
And ask His promised peace in days of trial,
Sufficient strength for all the ways I go.

So in my second childhood I shall seek Him,
And strive to trust Him till my latest breath.
Then shall I wake, beyond the passing shadows,
And learn at last that life is reached through death.

LEARNING

God spoke at twilight; 'Now is time to learn
The last hard lessons of your mortal life;
Renunciation, pain and weariness;
The fret of others' weakness, and your own.'
This I accept. Could it be otherwise,
Far up the mountain, winter coming on?
But what constricts my heart with more dismay
Is the remembrance of the wasted years,
The earlier, easy lessons scarce half-learnt;
Failings unmastered, dreams unrealised,
The many, many things I meant to do.
'Father,' I cried, 'old age has come too soon.'

You spoke of many mansions, Lord;
Lord Jesus, promise me
You will find room for those who are still
Learning their A, B, C.

SUN'S JOURNEY

Softly, at daybreak, light touched the trees,
Waking birds to song and mankind to labour;
At noon, the sun stood high above the woodland, casting
Bright, golden spears to earth.

At sunset, rays were diffused and gentle;
Each leaf lent its colour to the lambent glow,
And the leaves of the tree caught the light in their mesh,
Till the tree and the light were one.

I too have come to the evening of life,
Seeking the peace of sunset, the soft shining;
Seeking the benison of God's light. Ah, when
Shall I and the light be one?

LEONARD T COLEMAN

I have written poems and monologues since my schooldays in Tunbridge Wells. I served in the Royal Air Force as a Tradesman Group I (instrument maker) (war service 5 years) - main career in Local Government - committee clerk writing minutes of meetings - then surveyor's chief clerk - a total of 44½ years if you include war years. I received a Queen's Jubilee Medal in 1977 for Long Service. I was for many years a semi-pro musician in dance bands around Tunbridge Wells and Medway towns, and secretary of my local NALGO, and secretary of my Tunbridge Wells branch of Musicians' Union. I have written lyrics and in my youth did announcing and vocals with dance bands. I retired in 1978 and tried painting in oils and water-colours, but resumed writing poetry as a pleasurable hobby and have been published quite a lot. My own first collection 'A Procession Of Words' was published in 1995 by Minerva Publishing, Knightsbridge, London. I was published in 'Starlit Dreams' by Spotlight poets and various other anthologies.

THE LOTTERY

Which are the numbers I must choose
To make that mystic set.
Six magic numbers that will make
The richest sequence yet.

How shall I reckon my slim chance
Of ending, in the frame.
The highs, the lows, the in-betweens,
Propelling one to fame.

Each tumbling ball is swirled around
Until the die is cast,
The swirling ending suddenly
They come to rest at last.

A pause, to drop into each place,
Their random order made.
A single turn which can suffice
And check each ball delayed,

Someone will win; if not today
Then on some new roll-over,
To change their lives - perhaps their wives;
Making new pigs in clover.

This man-made gamble that we see
Just adds another tumble;
Across the rocky road of life
Along which we must stumble.

THE CARDBOARD CITY

A product of our time, the Cardboard City
Assembled nightly, in each small arcade.
Against the wall, beside the ornate lamppost
The modern vagrants there whose beds are laid,

The regulars, beneath their newsprint coverlet,
Surrounded by their dirty crumpled gear,
Epitome of depths of human debris
Perpetuated each night of the year

Whose ages range across the several life spans,
From early youth to senile self-decay.
The drop-outs, and the destitute, - mere children,
Whose only crime it was - to run away

How can you help such truly helpless people,
So many choosing just this sort of way,
Living on charity, and scrounging handouts,
From anyone who is prepared to pay.

This is the other side - the obverse coinage,
Of everything that made this Britain great.
A desperation born of easy living.
The curse affecting every welfare state.

The old, old, children's story, surely,
Reminiscent - grasshopper and ant,
Blaming a hypocritical poverty
Merely a wicked sanctimonious cant.

When surely youth could rise against such horror,
And stand once more on its two healthy feet.
To banish once for all this modern squalor
That desecrates our every town and street.

THE LOVE SEAT

Two lovers sitting on a bench
In New York's Central Station.
It could be London, Paris, Rome,
Or any such location.

A man, a woman, naturally
Attracted to each other.
As old as time, as young as rhyme,
It could be dad and mother

For this is love in springtime
When our old world starts re-living
With Valentines, and daffodils,
And all the joys of giving.

To rediscover romance,
Maybe faded in September.
To bloom again this season
That all lovers still remember.

And seek again the lovers' bench
To hold hands in the park.
Or in some other trysting-place,
When twilight fades to dark.

Or in the morning sunlight
Their lives blossoming anew.
With whispered words of love
And hope, to make their dreams come true.

LOVE

What is love, I wish I knew,
A bond that has no gender.
It seems, an element of which
Is always warm and tender.

A friendship more than most
Which must include a deep affection.
Its purest form - a man and woman's
Choice - natural selection,

Directed to each other when
They find a mutual trust.
Their admiration mingling
With elements of lust.

To drift out time together,
In a marriage of their living.
Bound by the law - or not at all
But sharing, and forgiving.

Forgetting self - ignoring health,
They come together trying.
Accepting poverty or wealth
With happiness or crying.

But spending every moment
With the deepest sense of caring.
Through all life's tribulations,
Births and deaths, without despairing.

Nor losing hope that this is something worth
Retaining,
The power-force of love
That motivates us, all-sustaining.

THE SURGEON

Unlike the poet, the surgeon is a skilled man,
Who wrestles with the fragile human clay.
To solve the problems poets merely write about,
Albeit, in their own especial way.
The surgeon has a job to do, concerned with every breath.
The poet only pens his lines, on life, and love, and death.

The surgeon is a kind man, whose skills have cut him deep,
Incisions and decisions, that deprive him of his sleep.
And yet I'm sure Almighty God is standing by his side,
And anxiously deliberating what he must decide.

Our thanks are due to both of them, our maker, and his mate,
Who do their best, regardless of that fickle partner, fate.
Making our life, and mending it, when things burst at the seams,
And sometimes even ending it, despite their hopes and dreams.

The gift of life is precious, and we owe so much to them.
Let no one lightly criticise, nor cynically condemn;
The surgeon's skill is manifest, the best hope you can find,
Of all the jobs he has the best, to love and save mankind.

He stands apart, and may seem therefore distant and aloof,
But he does care, as I declare - I am the living proof.
A lonely job, with little thanks - he has no time to dream,
But honoured by his fellow men, and high in our esteem.

THE BRITISH CONSTITUTION

The British Constitution is a model for the world.
The rule of law our peoples saw when freedom's flag unfurled.
Unwritten, but emphatic, unambiguous and free,
And standing proud - above the crowd - defending you and me.

The mother of all parliaments to represent our cause,
To champion the underdog, and supplement our laws.
Whose voice is heard in every land our argument to press,
And do that which is possible - injustice to redress.

From early Greek, from Roman law, and every Saxon thane,
This model form of government will triumph yet again.
For history is our defence the birthright of us all;
So stand erect - do not defect -
As Britishers walk tall.

Invasions, wars, and pestilence we have withstood them all,
But European Union is a more insidious call,
So stand together countrymen in this new hour of need,
The House of Lords must draw the swords they sheathed
At Runnymede.

Let everyone be on their guard against this 'tender trap'
Which offers bland inducements tossed into a willing lap.
It's time for us to stand and man the beaches once again,
Or else our island heritage will all have been in vain.

ROBERT GRAVES - POET 1895-1985

I stood on a hill in Majorca,
That island of soft cloudless skies.
Just one tiny churchyard, in summer,
Made famous, where Robert Graves lies.

His grave - just a slab of plain concrete,
No doubt it was locally made,
Crudely scribed with a stick, on the grass slope,
Under which he was reverently laid.

A simple rough tablet - thus fashioned,
Seems less than enough for this man,
Who sleeps there beneath it at Deya,
Where he loved, and lived out his life's span.

So distant, remote from the turmoil,
That characterised his spent youth.
The mud, and the carnage, of Flanders,
His manhood, and pursuit of truth.

DEPARTURES

Sharing the tears, the sorrows, nervous laughter,
Standing upon the platform of our dreams.
Waving away our innermost emotions,
Shattering the ecstasy of plans and schemes.

Looking into each other's eyes - that glisten
Wondering if, or when, we'll ever meet,
Making the effort not to hurt each other
By saying something rash, or indiscreet.

this is the precious language of departure,
Sadly translated on life's devious track.
Hoping, where hope has died, for resurrection
Of our great love, that has no turning back.

THE OLD ELM TREE, AT HOVERINGHAM

There was a small hotel I knew
Beside the River Trent,
Below the base, at Syerston,
High - on its escarpment.

Where wooded slopes looked down, upon
Green water-meadows bare,
The sweeping river-bend - the mighty Trent,
That flowed through there.

Placid in summer, flooding
In winter, to divide,
And isolate The Old Elm Tree Hotel,
On either side.

It was from Syerston we came,
From Bingham, for the boat,
A cockleshell contraption,
Upon which we used to float.

Across the rushing river,
A full sixty yards or more,
To reach the wooden landing-stage
Upon the further shore.

Endangered in the winter's dark,
Or when the fog came down,
By heavy-laden barges too,
From some great Northern town.

The landlord's name was Norman,
An ex-borstal warden, he,
Despite an artificial leg,
Performed efficiently.

He'd sit back in the stern
A single oar was all he'd need,
To skilfully manoeuvre in between
Each bunch of reed.

He rowed - electric motor powered
By an ancient 'ACC',
Provided by the Air Force,
And they didn't want it back.

I made the journey regularly
Standing in the bow,
Ready to jump and fix the rope,
And keen to show them how.

In time of flood it's difficult
To judge the water's flow,
And if you miss your footing
In the river you will go.

To cause much laughter at the time,
But I was quickly dried,
Beside an open fire - and whisky
Helped restore my pride.

I was a valued customer,
The leader of the band,
And played for nearly two years
On that simple rostrum stand.

My instrument, the saxophone,
A pianist and drummer,
We played the weekly dances,
Through the winter and the summer.

We played at weddings, birthdays,
And for many a celebration,
Whenever duties would allow us
From our service station.

The people came from Nottingham
In war-time - from all sources,
With boys and girls from factories,
And always, all the Forces.

Full many a romance blossomed
On those summer riverbanks,
The place where I spent many hours
Of playing, to all ranks.

But now, alas - I understand
Even the elm tree's gone,
The pub replaced by people's flats,
Its charm and glamour done.

But there are many of us
Will not easily forget
That place, where we found happiness
Is always with us - yet,

The changes - all apparent,
As relentless time is spent,
With memories of the old elm tree
Beside the River Trent.

KIRAN SHAH

I was born in Nairobi, Kenya on 28 September 1956 and stayed there till I was ten. In Kenya my parents had to work hard but we had a comfortable and a happy life. I then moved to India for one year where I saw a lot of sufferings and hardships. I witnessed people struggling just to survive, unlike Kenya. I then moved with my parents to London which was a complete contrast. I completed my O'Levels and decided to take up acting as my career because of my height 4ft 1in.

In 1973 I got my first break in Red Buddha Theatre working as a mime artist. For the next four years I appeared in various experimental theatres as a mime artist. In 1976 I got my first work in a film 'Candle Shoe' as a stunt artist. Since then I have been appearing in movies, television and commercials as an actor or doing stunts. Some of the films I have worked in are 'People That Time Forgot', 'Raiders of the Lost Ark', 'Legends', 'Bull's Eye', 'The Crucifier of Blood', 'The Adventures of Baron Munchausen'.

Having lived in three different continents I have seen a lot of contrast in the lifestyles of people from region to region and mistrust between people from different countries. This has raised lots of questions in my mind which leads me to write poems to let my feelings and opinions out. I have been influenced by song writers like John Lennon, George Harrison, Bob Dylan and Sting with their lyrics about the world situation. Also the word-play by poets like Dylan Thomas and Sylvia Plath have had an influence.

I also want to thank my father Jethalal Shah who passed away in 1995, my mother Mukta Shah and my brother Hasmukh Shah and his wife Manjula Shah for their support and encouragement to write poetry.

SHADOW

Shadow of mine,
Kept following me,
Wherever I went.
Every time looking down,
At my shadow.
I kept wondering,
What it would be like,
To be a shadow?

I was a shadow of a man once,
Kept following him
Wherever he went.
Sometimes it would be a tough trip,
Sometimes it would be a calm walk.
I hated bumping onto the rocks,
Or half bending on the walls.
There was always a pain,
Getting run over by a car.
All the people and animals,
Kept treading on me,
There was never peace.

Every time I look down,
At my own shadow,
I keep wondering,
How painful it is,
To be somebody's shadow.

FORGOTTEN HERO

The knife struck him deep suddenly.
His face expressed horror and surprise.
His mouth wide open as though in a scream.
The fear grew in his eyes,
As he fell to the ground staring.

To the open blue sky
With specks of white clouds floating.
His life projected on to the clouds.
His brain goes wild with thoughts.
He wants to say a lot
But the wind carries no sound.

Slowly and silently
His mouth closes in vain.
His eyes begin to fall asleep.
He lies there in a smile,
As the wind rises high,
They carry him away.

Next day, mourners gather together.
Mourning in sorrow for a great loss,
For he was a fighter.

Pity fills their heart.
Talk of his good deeds spread,
For in their eyes
He was a hero - a saviour,
Who died like a man.

Tears flow freely everywhere.
As many hear of his tale,
But soon the last of the mourners leaves,
And he is forgotten.

Today
Nobody remembers to put flowers
On his grave.

PIE IN THE SKY

The sun floats high in the sky,
Burning the desert sand to golden brown.
Temper raises in the heat of the moment.
Not seeing race creed or colour.
Religion and sanity goes out of the window,
Like the wind blowing in the desert wind.
All the wars and hatred towards each other,
In the name of religion and race to see.
It tears my heart open in pieces,
To see empty spaces in their eyes.
Abandoning ethics of the great teachings,
To score one over for his name's sake
Making a hero out of this crime,
Behind the closed doors glorifying them to the one.

Super-power's all want to be that glory,
Fighting for so-called rights in his name.
Flaunting the law of mother nature for thy glory,
Dirtying his name for glorification high pie in the sky.
Forgetting the feeling of this mother nature,
Hurting her right in her throbbing heart.
Red blood flows like a volcano of love,
From the slender round body of love.
Emptying spaces of non-habitation places to breathe in,
Fleeing, running, finding places to hide the one.
Fighting must go on in his name to win,
To grab the power of guilt in his name.
Wanting it all in the vision of his peace,
Shattering that vision in the name of peace.
Life begins to dictate for that pure greed,
To grab for that pie in the sky.

Is there any justice in what we are doing,
Is there a point in this reason to live or die for.
Be free to yourself like the wind riding the horse,
Surrender yourself to the wind and his teaching.
You can be anything in his name . . . free,
You can give anything your heart desires . . . free.
Destroy your fear and darkness will lift,
Like the wind it will blow from the soul.
The quest you seek will be the real pie in the sky,
Grab it with both hands free to see.
Trusting your soul in his name to free,
To win to lose is not all lost to see.
One can reach high to the floating sun,
Then his justice will fall on you,
Freeing the true gifts of the universe created,
In the heart of hearts of a thousand souls.
There is no time left anymore for us,
The chances we have lost over and over.
Who wants to live forever,
When you've got everything in his goodness.

Till the end of time.

UNIVERSAL PRAYER

The great Lord of this universe
What Thy name we call
Krishna, Mahavira, Buddha, Adonai, Jesus, Allah
We pray to You with a name.
Have pity in Thy heart,
For all the life forms in Thy universe.
Show us the way,
For peace and unity.
With Your love for all Thy life
That You have created
In Thy universe.

BORROWED TIME

This universe, this galaxy, this solar system
Moves to infinity from the source of the bang.
New stars created, as old ones die,
In all the galaxies as they form and die.
In this time that is borrowed time.

This past, this present, this future
Moves to infinity from the source of the bang.
As now the time is set in motion
As the past time moves in history dead.
In this time that is borrowed time.

This soul, this body, this life-form
Moves to infinity from the source of the bang.
New life created, as old ones die out.
This soul moves to a new body forever.
In this time that is borrowed.

TASTED

I have tasted freedom.
I have tasted love.
I have tasted hatred.
I have tasted calmness.
I have tasted anger.
As I have lived in these
The material life.
These are the five elements
One has to live through
To fit in to so-called society
In order to survive the everyday life.

But now,
I truly want freedom,
To truly understand love.
I truly want hatred,
To truly understand calmness.
I truly want anger,
To truly free myself
Of this life and all lives.
To understand, to be part of
This whole universe, to be
As equal as all the stars as one.

FAIR MAIDEN

I think of thee
Even in my sleep
As a vision of love
I long to see and touch
My heart beats greatly

Fair maiden
You came
Fair maiden
Thee
Fair maiden.

Alas I feel fright
To be mine love
For the fear of
As a friend
I torment in

To ask you
Fair maiden
Losing you
Fair maiden
My mind.

Only a wish of you
Would be granted
The wish would be of you
My heart is of devotion
I love thee
But from afar.

Fair maiden
I wish
Fair maiden
Of you
Fair maiden

THE THOUGHTS IN DEPRESSION

I sit in the corner,
Dark clouds cover my mind.
As I sway from side to side,
Thousands of thoughts attack the brain.
A thought never lasting a minute
Incomplete glowing and fading.
Which string to follow gets complicated,
Death and life, life and death,
Going round and round in circle.
Cannot make up my mind
Where to begin
Where to end.
Is this all worth it?
To live for, to die for,
I cannot make a complete picture,
Or what to do next.
Whether to move, leave my corner,
A decision is nearly there,
But then vanishes like a flash.
Confused, isolated I sit numb
In my cosy corner,
As I sway from side to side.

THE STORM

The wind that lashes out in scorn
Has anger like no fury
Falling everything in its path
The rain that falls with a force
Like a waterfall drowning
Everything in its path.

Has anger like no fury,
Millions of lives suffer
The shelter of houses or forests
No longer safe in this fury
Washed away like matchsticks
Swept up, flown across
Everything in its path
Up the skies with no control.

Millions of lives suffer
In this season that's changed
The perfect winter, perfect spring,
The perfect summer, perfect autumn,
Changed unintentionally in this
The wind that lashes out in scorn.

IF

Like Lennon said,
In his song 'Imagine',
Now would not that be
A dream to strive for.

If there were no boundaries,
If there were no cast,
If there were no religions,
If there were no colours,
If there were no wars,
If only if.

Like Lennon said,
In his song 'Imagine',
Would not that be
A dream to strive for.

If there was only unity,
If there were same laws,
If there was same equality,
If there was same freedom
If only everyone lived together,
In the brotherhood,
If only if.

Like Lennon said,
In his song 'Imagine',
Would not that be
A dream to strive for.

WISDOM

As the saying goes that,
At the prime of life,
The wisdom of life comes.
One matures like a fine wine
As we get older and experienced.
But that wisdom is,
A little bit too late.
As the young don't listen,
They think they know the life.
Then it would be nice to
Have that wisdom when young.
Then one can set up the goals,
Achieve everything in life to be.
That is when we need,
This wisdom most.
So that our life will go
Accordingly to what we planned.

PEGGY HUNTER

Peggy Hunter was born in a small town on the outskirts of Leeds. She attended a church infant/junior school and the local council school, leaving at the age of 14 years. She continued her education with 4 years of evening classes. Peggy's working life was spent in various clerical positions. For the last twenty years of her working life Peggy was a Hire and Sales Controller for a company in the construction service industry.

Peggy has two sisters, both married with families. Peggy was married in 1947, her husband Ted had served in the Navy during the war but was discharged with a disability pension. Peggy's husband died in 1987, they did not have any children.

Peggy enjoys sequence dancing and gardening. Writing poems has always been an interest but this interest developed after Peggy became a widow.

A group (including Peggy) went on a dancing holiday. The organiser decided to have an Old Time Music Hall theme on the last evening. This lady had a dream and in it Peggy recited poetry. They came to the conclusion that this event must have occurred fifty years earlier when they were both at school.

This spurred Peggy on to produce poems of her own to go with the recitations and her writing of poetry has continued up to the present time.

Peggy now shares her home with three cats and is sometimes inspired to write about them. Other topics in her work include day to day happenings and past experiences. Peggy has had a number of poems published in various magazines and anthologies, also in a small book of her own work 'Quiet Moments'. She once read one of her poems on Radio Leeds and has read some of her poems in the Morley Public Library.

PERCHANCE TO DREAM

Some nights when you lay in your bed
Sleep seems very far away
You toss and turn and wait for dawn
Wishing it was next day

You think of funny things from the past
Maybe try counting sheep
It seems the harder that you try
You're further away from sleep

You hear the old tunes on the radio
Then the news on the hour is read
You hear it at two, and three, and four
Why can't you sleep in your bed

I go to the kitchen, make cups of tea
Look out of the window at the quiet drive
Think of the lovely dreams I am missing
As to go to sleep I strive

Some things cost lots of money
But sleep is one thing that's free
As you toss and turn around in your bed
You think, why doesn't it happen to me

Then finally away you go
Perhaps have some pleasant dreams
Morning will soon bring another day
All too soon it seems

So for all the sleepless people
I will say a little prayer
That sleep will soon be with you
And you will rest without a care.

MONDAYS

Monday's not our washing day
But our day to visit the dales
For seven years now, in all kinds of weather
Our enjoyment of these trips never fails

Now that we've retired
We three ladies have this Monday treat
Armed with cameras, flasks and sandwiches
A pastime hard to beat

Wharfedale, Swaledale, Wensleydale
Each beautiful in its own special way
The views, the grazing animals
All add lustre to our day

Goathland where they film *Heartbeat*
Askrigg for *All Creatures Great and Small*
Kilburn to see the White Horse on the hill
Or Aysgarth for the waterfall

To markets, old towns and castles
Country houses or a village fair
Picnics by lakes and rivers
Church flower festivals, we'll be there

Over the moors on a steam train
Or follow winding lanes to places far
Up the hills and down the dales
Travelling by car

We have a very good driver
Who usually knows the right way
Then when tired with all our sight-seeing
Brings us home safely at the end of the day.

AN AGE-OLD PROBLEM

The road ahead seems to divide
It's hard which path to take
You want to choose the right one
A difficult decision to make

Should you try sheltered housing
Leave your own home, a big step to take
Stay on your own, not well, very lonely
So very much at stake

This house is your home, your memories are here
Perhaps the wrench to leave it too great
But have you overstayed your welcome
It seems large and cheerless, what is your fate

Often help is offered
We can't always be pleased to accept
People mean well, but their ways
Are not always what we would expect

Our body seems to be wearing away
But our mind, to us seems the same
With creaking bones and fading sight
It's not easy to see what is plain

If we could hear well that would be a help
But that's a problem too
Why can't we feel as we did at sixteen
With parts all shiny and new

But knowledge gathered over the years
Should help us in our task
The best road to a peaceful retirement
Is really all that we ask.

THE OLD BLUE CASE

I like to go to Auntie's house
She keeps an old blue case
Full of clothes for dressing up
Bits of ribbon and lace

Long dresses, bangles, strings of beads
Lace curtains to dress like a bride
Scarves, earrings, long gloves
Lots more odd things besides

I get dressed up, then twirl around
Think how nice I look
Just like a fairy princess
From my favourite storybook

When I get to be a grown-up
I'll have my own blue case
Full of lovely odds and ends
And things to paint my face

Then maybe other children
Will call on me to see
The treasures in my old blue case
And dress up just like me

LIFE IN THE FAST LANE

Why is it that some people
Find it hard just to unwind
Shake off life's worries and troubles
Leave them all far behind

Tension and nail-biting moments
Seem to be all that they know
No chance to rest and recharge their batteries
Always on the go

Pressure from their daily life
Like chains holding them fast
Futures unpredictable
Clash with phantoms from the past

Sometimes when we worry
The problem only seems to increase
We find no answer to the question
Our mind can find no peace

We should know we shall be given strength
For the tasks we must do today
Tomorrow's needs must take their turn
When dawns another day

THOUGHTS OF FIRST LOVE

The wind whistles down the chimney
The bushes sway and dance
Leafless branches cavort on the trees
Not a morning to think of romance

Yet I sit here and think of my first love
Walking hand in hand by a stream
Thoughts only of each other
A kiss stolen, as if in a dream

No thoughts too far into the future
Wrapped up in the world of our own
There is nothing to compare with a first romance
It has a magic for us alone

After a while we drifted apart
Even good things do not last
What brought back these thoughts today
Memories from the past

Perhaps it's a sign of growing old
That was fifty years ago
The winds of time have stirred my memory
And the gale continues to blow.

QUIET MOMENTS

As I sit spending quiet moments
Or sometimes when lying in bed
Not thinking of anything in particular
Various thoughts come in my head

Sometimes the thoughts are happy
Depending upon the day
Others they are sad or wistful
As I while my time away

Now I write them all down in my notebook
Before they are lost for all time
The words seem to tumble out over each other
And usually manage to rhyme

I just write of things as I see them
Day to day happenings or things from times past
My hobby gives me much pleasure
And my notebook is filling up fast.

ST PETER'S KEYS

The cowslip, a fragrant yellow flower
We expect to herald the spring
Now suffering demise, since I was a child
No more joy to our hedgerows to bring

The oxslip from 'A Midsummer Night's Dream'
Probably the same flower
Its multi-head and pale green leaves
Once clothed our banks after each April shower

Some call it St Peter's Key
Based on legend or an old wives' tale
Say when St Peter was unlocking the Pearly Gates
He stumbled, causing his grip to fail

His keys tumbled down to reach the earth
Separating as they floated and fell
Each one turning into a lovely flower
The cowslip we know so well

This flower has always been special to me
Hope each spring it continues to grow
Perhaps St Peter will guard it
That's something we'll never know

A FAREWELL DRINK

The funeral was over
Last respects had all been paid
A few sad tears, all timely shed
White lace-edged hankies all displayed

They went back to the departed's house
For sandwiches and tea
And a little friendly family chat
That is how it seemed to me

Then, who will have that lovely vase
I've always admired it so
Or the little oak table in the hall
Does anybody know

Do you think they will sell the house
Or leave it to someone here
I wonder how much is in the bank
I feel shocked at what I hear

Then someone is approaching
There is a knock at the door
It is a man with a briefcase
Of his name I was not sure

He seems to be carrying something else
And as he steps inside
He appears to be carrying a large bottle
Which he is trying to hide

He asks if he can have some glasses
And will people please take a seat
He pours everyone a large whisky
Then gets to his feet

He says will they please have a drink
To bid the departed goodbye
He thanks them all for coming
And asks them not to cry

He then takes out the will to read
You could have heard the drop of a pin
Everyone wondering, who will get what
He starts reading, his face rather grim

You seldom came to visit me
Though you are all here today
I don't know how you planned to spend my cash
Once I am out of the way

I know you've all had busy lives
In which I had no place
But five or ten minutes now and then
You could have shown your face

But I've never been alone
I have had my furry friend
Always loving and faithful
Right to the very end

After much consideration
As I sat for hours on my own
I have spoken to my solicitor
And left the lot to the Cats' Home

They looked at each other with shocked surprise
Did not know what to think
Then someone said 'Please pass that whisky,
We all need another drink.'

RECOLLECTIONS FROM MY CHILDHOOD

When a child only five years old, a happy holiday I spent
Eyemouth just over the Scottish border, this is where I went

I stayed in a large and square white house
That looked over the harbour and sea
It was a pretty fishing village
And must have left its mark on me

Some sixty years later I came with a friend
To retrace my steps would be fine
There was the house just as I remembered it
I seemed transported to some other time

In this house you can go through the fireplace
To tunnels which lead to the sea
Used in the past by smugglers
So no prying eyes could see

I remember the fishing nets drying in the sun
The floats which I thought to be balls
Wanting them, then having a large ball bought
Hearing the seagulls' calls

Seeing ladies cleaning large piles of fish
Not liking the sight or the smell
These were the herring caught by the fishermen
Being prepared for them to sell

I remember swallowing a hard-boiled sweet
Then needing to find a cool drink
Climbing on a chair to reach the tap
Getting my socks wet as I stood in the sink

I am pleased I came back to Eyemouth
To relive part of my childhood days
The memories have flooded back over the years
I hope they stay with me always

BRAD GRIME

I was born in Essex, Colchester. I was adopted at nine years old.

I started writing poetry at the age of sixteen after watching the movie 'Platoon'. Most of my early poems were written as a way out, the best way to express feelings. I have no real influences in writing poetry but I did like the Narnia series, Rosemary Sutcliff, Mary Stuart and Michael Crighton. I love movies ever since I watched 'Star Wars' at the age of seven.

What I see around me I try to write. 'Cattle Train' was written for a course project at College. I am on an Access Course hoping at some stage to go to College.

I was a forester for eleven years and now I wish to try my hand at writing. The world is my desk and what I see is what I see.

I really just like to write poetry, I have just completed a poem on 'Titanic'. At present the only thing that keeps me back is lack of words.

STONES OF AGES

Lichen scarred and brash limestone,
cracked and fissured, old and full of adventure,
intertwined with a gleam of polished olive ivy.
Clinging relentless, drinking the bind of stone,
holding upright, firm with meaning.
A story can be told from rock, stone and ballast.
Castles and knights,
cannonballs and civil fights,
down with monasteries, Saxon and Henry alike.
Smashed and ground to dust,
a story or legend we entrust.
Knowledge we can find,
history way behind,
an adventure, a history: a pyramid divine.

TRAMP

Mooching and moaning, the old grump sighing.
A weathered box residing,
Sainsbury's.
His home for a few weeks or years,
every day seeming to merge into one.
A disused garage leaking,
rusting tin and bent.
A halfway door
Broken by bored truant kids.
Bearded and tatty scarf, help to hold back the cold.
Haggard and weather-worn,
bruises from a kicking some time ago,
yellow.

ROOFLESS HOME

Splattered with rain,
cans and bottles, left carelessly.
The stinking wretches on benches.
Rotting food taken from bins.
A pride and joy of collected cans in Kwik Save trolley.

Drink more, drink more.
Drunken their legs asunder.

The asking of money,
'Can ya spare some change?'
a common occurrence
'God bless ya,'
or English verbal disasters, swearing.

Smoke more, smoke more,
keeping the hearth inside warm.

The blatant blackmail of young girls,
with sorrowful eyes, of babies beside them.
Knowing not what goes on,
just tired and hungry.
Innocent, of innocence deprived.
Does one fall into the trap
Or fall headlong feeling crap?

Hopelessly hopeless.
Devouring all souls who enter.

Circumstances of paths entwine,
young girls, women and men decline.
Freedom from taxes and mortgages,
paid highly in full,
by the solitude of warmth.

The street people,
a crying bloody shame?

PIRATE

As the onslaught of waves are breached,
the torrential torrent of forbidding rain rages.
Smashed masts and broken heads.
Oncoming onward never seeking refuge,
wildly pursued by magistrate and foe.
Left-over sail, bellowing through a polka-dot starry sky.
The flaring of a defty designed cannon gouging holes,
ensuring ghastly endeavours come to hand.
Those bloody bloody pirates now smuggled upon pointed rocks,
like miscellaneous pebbles, small and insignificant.
No more will they fight, the Spanish, the English and the pirate.

SUPERMARKET

The bantering of women through a shop store.
Scatterbrained till girl, new to the job.
'Have you heard what Mrs so and so said?'
'No' comes the reply to all ahead.
Listening on, she does waffle.
The till girl alloyed,
holding up traffic.
Comes a funny look,
till girl replying 'Would you mind moving because the rest are static.'
Shuffling on, one by one.
The girl now ready to quit,
had a long day and not really that fit.

DAYS OF PAPER

A blank piece of paper,
A nightmare for writers.
As one is born, a blank page.
Day by day a single word emerges.
As one grows up, the paper grows longer.
Some words get crossed out.
Forgotten days increase.
People lose words and days forever it seems.
Forever is a long time.
Misplacement of words or days will always remain,
For some they will never find them even in eternity.
Even memories fade with time.
A piece of paper will fade its words with age.
The piece of paper remains, slightly tarnished.

A PINBALL CHRISTMAS

Pinball shopping, bumping into everybody.
Bags, babies, baskets and bamboozlement.
Christmas madness. Christmas tidings,
never minding the pocket, now full of holes.
Christmas cheer. Christmas fear, laughter and grumpiness.
Frumps, pumps and angora sweaters,
keeping warm, not a hard decision.
Precision is all that is needed.
Cards, parcels and sleigh bells ringing.
Ding-a-ling-a-ping-pong, a pinball we all be.

CONNECTING ROAD

The green of the meadow,
the hay to feed the beasts.
The golden gaze of corn,
to feed, man, woman and child.
To hunger is unforgivable;
greed is unattainable.

The roads of ancient,
ponder through mud, muck and hole.
Connecting cities far and far.
To wander such desperate roads,
thieves go about their pillage, stealing riches,
ungiving, brutal, fearful and true.

With the woods surround and without sound,
The road excreting entrails by the wayside,
Drawing battling armies to enrage.
Battled blood draining through shingle and sand,
The road mingling blood with mud, muck and hole,
leaving empty child-like carcasses behind.

Why child cry so?
Sat beyond rotten stump and putrid carcasses.
Marching armies caressing the water-filled footholes of the road,
march, march, trudge, trudge, all of them tin-canned soldiers.
The cries of hurdled combatants dispersed,
their echoes haunting the holes in the road.

Upon yonder path,
soldiers arm to do battle untold,
the force, the steel undetermined.
Wives, mistresses and whores alike,
their men, fight, fight, fight.
A child crying, for want of a cradle. A creation of war.

As fortune soldiers quarry their foe,
The forgotten rations now embraced with maggot and worms,
The questioning, moralities and blindness,
Disembodied, disembowelled, devout Christians all.
Tainted plates of armour rusting rivets with blood,
the women, widows and the children fatherless.

To hanker for peace, a foolish errand,
the crying, the wailing, to no end.
God created the earth; man created war!
Families destroyed, worn down, tired, hungry and clothes threadbare.
War doesn't care, doesn't respond to love,
it is, without doubt, relentless.

The bloody, bloody meadow,
the greying hay not fit for beasts.
The red glaze of corn,
unfit to feed, man, woman and child.
To thirst is unforgivable,
inner peace is unattainable.

GOOD MORNING BRIGHT

Stars of bright
Gaining forever height
Endless travelling beyond our sight
But never outdoing the sun's might
The tranquil tranquil such a delight
As the sun rises from the night
Waking the morning with all its light.

COAL

Black, bleak and thorough,
the long tunnels of coal.
The dimly look of rickety supports,
wooden and roughly cut off square.
The apprehensive helmets of light,
plunging ever deeper by hand and pick.
Neighing ponies,
bred small and strong.
Their colours blackened,
sodden with soot.
Blinding blinkers to send them forward,
harnessed to the cart of coal.

CATTLE TRAIN

The seemingly endless, dark marauding train rolls in,
cattling people into cars, losing sight of the Star of David.
Frightened and despairing, drifting into the unknown.
Rattling and clanking, the rumble of the train.
Unmarked, uncaring, unsuspecting, even the train doesn't know.
'Where are we going?'
The questions are asked and unanswered,
the use of a baton to curb the barrage of questions.
Star of David, Star of David, provide us hope.

WOMANKIND

Wandering aimlessly through the world.
Never knowing what to expect.
A homely woman perceives life
very different from a hundred years past.
Washerwoman, wsherwoman, unrevered,
sometimes treated below life itself.

Women in charge, corporations to countries beyond.
Everywhere, everywhere now they belong.
Out of home, shaking the cloak of children.
Freedom, now conquering man at his own selfishness.

HURT KNEE

Avenues of blossom cherry.
A child's bike laying,
on two day old cut grass.
A gentle breeze blows,
scattering petals silently.
The front wheel still turning,
slowing down.
Tears rolling down her cheeks,
splashing down on her pink cardigan.
Holding tight her knee.
Hurting, grazed and bloody.

WARM MOON

Black rocks immersed in a salt-water glaze,
a velvet white virgin dress with a caress of down feathers.
A moonlight shade, outshone only by burgundy-coloured cheeks.
The wind brewing, warm, affectionate and allowing carefree hair
                                                        to blow.
A swelled sea boiled by the wind raising the froth and globules
                                                of water to waste.
The moonbeams and the glare of white water enhancing pictures
                                        ever present in dreams.

WHO ARE WE?

Wondrous sights 'n' sounds,
A demanding world enriches.
All souls, races and colour.
The cultural experiences emerge,
Causing tension and death.
Is it us
Or are we a game of chess,
For aliens above?
If aliens are playing,
It could explain black and white.
If not,
Surely it is us.
Who are we to judge?
We all could be pawns.
Yet we all could be kings and queens.
Maybe we are the aliens,
And the things we destroy are ourselves.

SPOOKED

Trembling anticipation, in the dead of night.
A boy awakes from a slumber.
Fallen asleep had he, many hours before.
It had been glorious sun.
Now awake, his trembling turned to fear,
For now he remembers why he was here:
To look at the citadels of stone,
Where lifeless souls rest.
Studying, preferably by day.
He was OK.
But at night!
Whilst awake, he'd swear . . .
Too many shadows, frightened of his own.
No noise, though he could hear the quiet of death.
Now walking tall, he'd had his fill.
Yelling out 'Enough is enough!'
Squeaking noise behind,
Startling him stiff,
First sound all night, save for heavy breathing.
The vicar was up and opening the gate.
Looking around slowly, hoping to wake.
Calling the vicar,
No sound did he make.
Disappearing and gone.
Vanished.

M JEPSON

I am a single 30-year-old father of one delightful daughter, Danielle Rebecca, aged nine. I was born in Batley and brought up and still live in Dewsbury, both of which are in West Yorkshire. I have worked most of my adult life as an electrician, also having had jobs as a kitchen assistant and for a very brief spell as a music promoter. I am now concentrating and learning more about writing.

Initially I started writing poetry as a therapy after a relationship split in 1991. Years went by and I didn't write anything until late 1996. This was a period of my life which was the worst, getting involved in crime and drinking huge amounts of alcohol.

After a brief spell in prison I decided to stop drinking and committing crime. Poems helped me through many lonely days and nights. Again they acted as a therapy. Poetry helps me put thoughts and feelings in black and white. It gives me a buzz when I consider I have written a decent poem.

I used to wait to be inspired in order to write about something until I read 'Don't wait for inspiration, look for inspiration!' That now is exactly what I do. I look for it in everything I do and others do and everywhere I go.

My poems can be put into five categories, crime and punishment, life stories, women, music and miscellaneous. Poems about everyday life and crime often are my main subjects, though not all are meant to be taken seriously.

THE ALMIGHTY WISH

God in heaven looking on down
seeing worried people with a constant frown
sending a message from way up high
wanting us to laugh and not to cry
you talk and talk and he lets you in
wishing people would smile and never to sin
laugh let's go down that path
laugh let's keep on that path

God in heaven up above
freedom flight of a peaceful dove
love of angels with a shining glow
God in heaven never feeling low
you talk and talk and he lets you in
wishing people would smile and never to sin
laugh let's go down that path
laugh let's keep on that path

God in heaven he created all
building confidence so we stand tall
not wanting hate just love and peace
but if he doesn't get these his love won't cease
you talk and talk and he lets you in
wishing people would smile and never to sin
laugh let's go down that path
laugh let's keep on that path.

BACK OF THE ROOM

the blackness in the sky
reflecting in your eyes
the blackness in the sky
reflecting in your eyes
I can't believe this moment
I can't believe it's true
I can't believe this moment
loving thoughts of you
I'm drifting on a piece of timber
this time I know where I'm going
a mirrored image of myself
respects are overflowing

did you see me stand at the back of the room
did you see me standing there
did you see me stand at the back of the room
I was the one with the silver hair
did you see me stand at the back of the room
I was all dressed in white
did you see me stand at the back of the room
I was such a heavenly sight

misty eyes that's no surprise
humming the tunes to the sound of the blues
are these the ones I choose
the sweetest smell of flowers
a new soul living I'm counting the hours
till I see your faces smile again
till I see your faces smile again
scuffled steps on hardened floors
men in black stand by wooden doors
drink a toast to my life before
I've got the gift of magic and plenty much more.

BROKEN PROMISE

you gave a broken promise to a broken child
you're looking for the answers you might never find
them here you don't have to fear
the actions of a running fallen man
he'll try and mess your mind up
but only if he can it's so clear you don't shed a tear

you gave a broken promise to a broken child
you're looking for a love you might never find
this year you can safely steer

through a few showers of mixed emotions
through a few flowers with scented potions
through a darkened sky with a misty haze
through a blackened eye of a worn-out phase

I will help you help you any way I can
I'll be there for you I will be your gentle man
I'll help you plan a rebirth of your life
with no more worries no more bloodied knife
I will help you help you any way I can

you gave a broken promise to a broken child
we're gonna mend the fences we're never gonna hide
from the happy time we'll never forget the crime
of a downtrodden man with his downtrodden life
crying the pain that he gave to his wife
with sneer you can safely cheer.

ELVIS

Elvis was known as the king of rock 'n' roll
according to a world-wide opinion poll
with his slicked-back hair and swaying hips
his guitar strumming and quivering lips
he's taken us down to a heartbreak hotel
rockin' 'n' rollin' in a jailhouse cell
loving us tender and telling daddy not to cry
loads of folk convinced he didn't really die
watching his films and all the girls within
singing to them with a cheeky little grin
Tulepo, Mississippi is where he was born
on August 16th true fans began to mourn
they were crying in the chapel and in the ghetto too
the Christmas of '77 was the colour of blue
Priscilla and Lisa he left behind
but I'm sure as for many he'll be
always on their mind.

LIES

why do we tell lies?
why don't we say what we mean?
why don't we say we hate?
instead of pretending to be keen
why don't we tell others when given the chance
instead of leading everyone in a crazy dance?
you don't really want to lie but people give you no choice
wishing you were only listening to a solitary voice
you want to do right by one and all
but you feel you're banging your head against a giant brick wall
I'm not gonna pretend I know where to go from here
'cos that's no lie, probably the first of the year.

SHE MAKES YOU LAUGH

she asked a question
what caught me off-guard
it wasn't that long
or really that hard

        'guess who I saw today?'
my mind went blank
I didn't know exactly what to say
with a gleam in her eye
a grin on her face
I was hoping for the answer
with severe haste
but she let me stew
for a second or two
it was brilliant
and off comes my hat
she replied jokingly
        'everyone I looked at.'

FUGITIVE

life on the run
it isn't always fun
moving from place to place
with such eager haste
people all around you not knowing
your real name
not wanting attention
not wanting the fame.

Sorrow

I'm sorry for missing the first steps you took
I'm sorry for missing words from the first book
I'm sorry for not being there when you needed me most
I'm sorry for not being there the first trip to the coast
I'm sorry for not being there to fix all your toys
I'm sorry for not being there to tell you about boys
I'm sorry for not seeing you for such a long time
I'm sorry for being in prison for committing a crime

'cos you're an angel
an angel from above
with your angelic smile
your world filled with love
you're an angel
you're an angel.

Alcohol-Free

every day in every way I am getting stronger
every day in every way my life is getting longer
I'm happier now than I was before
but then I let the devil through my door
he was dressed in black and he had a grin
God knows where he came from or where he'd bin
he spoke so softly and never raised his voice
he offered me a drink of any damned choice
but the devil juice can take its toll
it can screw you up and destroy your soul.

A LIFE

drowning in sorrowed drink
in a shell of a body
on a cloud of mistrust and deceit
loyalty no longer
confidence growing shorter
pains of the past haunting the mind
superb memories fizzling out
evil thoughts coming to the fore
the present can't be the past
nor the future be as great
the sadness of the eyes
the hurt of pride
the sorrow for so many
the torture of the soul
isolation is preservation of good
but the madness is seeping out
the voice of reasoning is of not real flesh
letting anger twist and turn
deep within the body
feeling the devil pain pushing
against the skin
delusional screenings flickering
back and forth
mute-filled crying with tear transparent
holding out a hand for no-one to be there
existing only for the sake of
a destiny too far
parting is all there is to do.

To Drink 'n' Drive

To drink 'n' drive is a dangerous thing
You're never quite sure what state you're really in
Even if you drink the legal limit of beer
Can you really be certain you can safely steer?
We're not all the same shape or the same weight
or digest food at the same old rate
You may have had a stressful day that's made you
feel tired and made you feel blue
But I can hear you now saying 'Who the hell are you?'
Well I'll tell you who I am shall I mate?
A man who had a couple of drinks and made myself late
I supped every last drop and put my glass on the bar
Walked through the door and straight into my car
Time was pushing on and I had my foot to the floor
I was like a man possessed trying to settle an old score
They said that little girl had only just come out to play
I put my brakes on, I heard a thud, I came to a halt
but there she lay, lifeless and still
with blood on her long blonde hair
It's wrong to think that I don't really care
and I deserved everything I got
From insulting names and finally being shot
So again I sit with my hands on the wheel
but in both legs I have no feel.

A PUBLIC MODEL

I sit down, I write my name
I know I'm not the one to blame
I stand up, I move around
knowing in my mind I'll be homeward bound
I sit down, stare at the floor
strange-looking people in and out of a door

I am a public model, a public model doing my job

I stand up, look straight ahead
muffled voices I can't hear what's being said
I'm told to move to number nine
I don't argue I think that is just fine
I step back, I don't smile
posing for a photograph to go on a file

I am a public model, a public model doing my job

I step forward to a brighten light
I won't be sleeping in a cell tonight
I stand still, no looking round
you can hear a pin drop there isn't a sound
four minutes pass it seems so long
they've picked number three now I think that is wrong

I am a public model, a public model doing my job

relief and joy for number two
wrongful arrest he could very well sue
I sign my name, collect my pay
all in all it's been a very good day

I was a public model, a public model doing my job

WHO ARE WE?

standing alone in a crowded town
hidden behind the happy is a constant frown
we follow the steps of the people of the past
we should all know that life goes too fast
we're living in the fast lane it don't
matter what speed you know
you put your foot on the pedal and try to brake slow
but you keep on going when it's time to go

do we know who we really are?
does anybody know who we really are?
living, eating, breathing, sleeping
does anybody know who we really are?

you look on down to the people who care
raining a stream of tears crying it's just not fair
life will go on for both them and you
but for disbelievers they won't have a clue
about a new soul living the way it was meant to be
an adventure playground you've paid your entrance fee.

DEBBIE CRAGGS

My name is Debbie Craggs; I live with my husband Bill, and two very special sons, Billy aged twelve and Peter aged seven, in an small ex-mining village Trimdon Grange.

As a child I grew up in another ex-mining village, Wheatley Hill. I was born on the 23rd July 1964 at Littlethorpe Hospital, Easington. Then I was a Beeston and very proud to be one.

My father not being with me when I was growing up, is what gave me the inspiration to write. There was no-one there to express how I really felt inside. I love to write as I can say what is going on inside my mind without anyone interrupting. I find poetry an easier way to release anger, painful memories, my views, and also to let people know just how much they mean to me.

Other than poetry, I love to listen to music, my favourite bands at present are Oasis, Pulp and The Verve with whom I can really relate. I don't like songs where the lyrics don't have a meaning. I'd love to meet Jarvis Cocker and Noel and Liam Gallagher to discuss their lyrics and for them to give an opinion on some songs I have written.

I suppose I'll write for the rest of my days. My younger son is following in my footsteps as he also likes to write poetry, whilst the eldest is more of a reader. I would like these poems to be dedicated to all my loved ones.

YOU STOLE MY YOUTH

My childhood dreams were torn in two,
With all the hell you put me through,
You allowed me to see what no child should,
Did you really think I was made of wood?
I'm not, I felt, I hurt, I also cried,
But love from you was always denied,
The times I've blamed myself, but I know
                                now that's not true,
As all the hell I've lived through
                                was all caused by you.
You sent away my dad, when it should have
                                been my brother,
What an evil person you really are,
you don't deserve the name 'Mother'.

TO BILL

Sometimes I find it hard to say,
The way I feel inside,
I want to tell you how much I care,
But my feelings from you I hide,

I'd really like to tell you,
The way you make me feel,
But the feelings of love I have for you,
Are so strong I can't reveal.

I've never felt like this before,
And again I never will,
As I believe you only love once,
My love is only for Bill.

FALSE APPEARANCES

Behind a face that laughs and grins,
A girl so sad is hidden within,
Gives the impression that she's so strong,
How appearances can be wrong,
Gives nothing away about the pain she feels,
All the hell that she's lived through is hard to reveal,
So much emotional pain she keeps locked up inside,
Nightmares she lives through, all the tears she's cried,
Violence and rape, she's lived through it all,
Her childhood memories aren't nice at all,
Keeping them hidden is really hurting her so,
I'm that girl and that's how I know.

THE JOURNEY

The journey along life's road is hard,
Especially if dealt a losing card,
You try so hard but no-one's impressed,
You start to think you've failed life's test,
You get back up and then you're knocked back down,
After a while you stay on the ground
Don't give up, gamble to win,
Have pride in yourself, don't give in,
Never give in to life's challenging test,
Get on with it, just do your best,
If you give it all you've got,
Then failed at life, you have not.

SUMMERTIME

Beside a pond, a bird is drinking,
His friends want to join, but they're still thinking,
The dog lies lazily in the sun,
Summertime has just begun.

The leaves on the tree, are waving at me,
Helped along, by the breeze from the sea,
The flowers are out, to put on a show,
It's summertime, they always know.

Children play happily, in every street,
To them summertime, is their annual treat,
Trips to the beach, McDonald's too,
England's so beautiful, who needs Corfu?

IF ONLY

If I could live my life over,
Then most things I would do the same,
I'd live both the good and the bad times,
But from my memory abolish all pain,

As all the bad times that we live through
Aren't nice but we always pull through,
But tears of pain always creep back,
They haunt us forever they do,

If we all lost all bad feelings,
And only remembered the good,
Then in love and harmony we all could live,
It would be heaven if only we could.

I HAD A DREAM

I had a dream, it was strange,
But it made me realise, that I must change,
As from today, I must start anew,
Do some things, I dream I do,

Now my children, are growing up,
I want a drink, from life's tasty cup,
For many years, with no time for a friend,
It's time for those days, to come to an end,

For others, I've always given up my time,
But now I'd like some time to call mine,
Bill loves me, the children do too,
I hope they respect, what I'd like to do,

I am a mother, who needs a break,
And that's what I, intend to take,
It may sound selfish, but that's how I feel,
The time has come to, make fantasy real,

For Bill and the boys, I am always here,
To love and protect them, show them I care,
I only hope, they don't begrudge me some time,
Some quality time, I can call mine.

DON'T NAG MAM

Here comes Peter, running so fast,
I'm pleased he's finally returned at last,
Where have you been? You've been gone so long,
Don't twist Mam, it's not long since I've been gone,

Here comes Billy, dawdling in,
Walks through the door, with his usual grin,
Billy do you realise it's almost dark,
Jesus Mam, I've only been to the park,

I don't want to nag, but they are my concern,
It's only I worry, will they ever learn?
For them to communicate, is my aim,
As life in the nineties, is a dangerous game,

I'd never forgive myself, if they got hurt,
As they're my responsibility, I'd feel like dirt,
I try to protect them, but they don't understand,
They mistake my love, for firm commands,

Maybe when they have kids of their own,
They will ask them, where they roam,
Only then, will they understand,
It was love, I gave, not commands.

DEDICATED TO LYNOTT BABY

Riding my horse, on a nice summer's day,
Seemed to take, all my worries away,
Lynott and I, trotting so fast,
People would admire her as we'd speed past,
She had the speed, plenty of spirit too,
I loved everything, that she would do,
A wild little filly, with plenty of go,
How I let them take her, I just don't know,
A wonderful trotter, with plenty of spirit,
God how I miss, my little Lynott,
I'd buy her back, if we had a field,
Then race on the track, as she had the speed,
Today no-one can ride her, the way that I could,
We understood one another, like horse and rider should,
She would not respond, to a whip or demands,
I'd talk to her pleasant, and she understands,
At that sight of a whip, she'd get on a high,
Whip my little Lynott baby, I'd rather die,
People still ask me all the time,
Where's your little trotter, that looked so fine?
My one wish in life, would be to have her back,
And show off her talent, out on the track.

PERFECTION

In the beginning, you were fragile and small,
But look at you now, so tall, so tall,
It's hard to believe, how small you were,
How you've matured, over the years,
Many times, I thought to give up on you,
As you looked so silly, as you grew,
Now so attractive to anyone's eye,
So ashamed of my thoughts now, I could die,
Look at you now, as you reach your prime,
I'm proud to say that you're one of mine,
You look so handsome, as you stretch to the sky,
Watching the birds, slowly pass by,
So attractive you are, and how you have grown,
I'm proud to say, our friendship is known,
Your beauty will now stay, for many a year,
No-one could harm you, they wouldn't dare,
You are so very special to me,
A perfect example of an oak tree.

I'VE BEEN TO HELL

You took away my self-respect,
Then stripped me of my pride,
You made me so afraid of you,
I ran from you to hide,

Years of pain you put me through,
But I won't take the blame anymore,
Perverts like you should be shot on sight,
So you can't rape no more.

DISPLAY NIGHT

Kids wrapped up like little bears,
Watching the fireworks, without any cares,
Multicoloured flashes, glow bright in the sky,
As exploding fireworks, go speeding by,
The smell of potatoes, chestnuts too,
Make our mouths water, as they cook through,
The flames from the fire, are burning so vicious,
Watching the kids, keeping them near us,

As the dying flames, turn to ash,
Another firework goes, *Boom! Bang! Flash!*
Then the crowds start slowly to drift away,
Kids cry out 'We want to stay,'
Parents reply with 'No,
It's almost bedtime, we must go,'
Off they go, with a sparkler in hand,
Obeying reluctantly, their parents' demands.

DÉJÀ VU

Do you ever get a feeling, as you open a strange door,
I can't remember being here, but I'm sure I've been before,
The pictures on the staircase, just don't refresh your mind,
But as you walk on further, strange happenings you find,
How do you know the rooms, when you've never been at all,
The bedroom with the fireplace, the round window in the hall,
How do I know you? Ask inside your mind,
Then a sudden urge to rush outside, as there's something you must find,
You rush out the side door, then round to the back,
Down a set of steps you go, open a door that's painted black,
There you find a little tin, you have seen before,
But how on earth did you know, where to find that black door?

WINTER ARRIVING

The gusting winds, howl in the night,
Birds move south, numerous in flight,
Leaves from the trees, dance around in the sky,
Clouds move so fast, as the wind blows them by,
The grass at a glance, looks like a stormy sea,
Twisting and turning, so wild, fast and free,
Dustbins clatter, as they are blown over,
Draughts come through windows, as winter gets closer,
Extra blankets, water bottles too,
A small tot of whiskey, to warm us through,
We all sit together, so cosy it's nice,
The pond outside, has a covering of ice,
There's a cat on the rocks, in hope of a fish,
But with the covering of ice, he'll just have to wish,
It won't be long now, till snow will appear,
It often arrives, at this time of year,
We all like to see snow fall in December,
Then when Christmas is over, we like it to end there,
Christmas is over, and here comes the sun,
Another year over, and a new one begun.

ALMOST TIME

Christmas cards, crackers and lights,
Little kids' faces, glow with delight,
Santa is coming, and we have to be good,
Or he'll fill our stocking with old rotting wood.

Mistletoe and holly, hung over the door,
Snow falls gently, and covers the floor,
Dad's singing carols, and Mam bakes mince pies,
Nobody likes them, but she always tries.

Christmas Eve, Dad puts on the lights,
A set that play carols, and flash so bright,
And some that flash different synchronised patterns,
And some light the tree, from inside little lanterns.

Tomorrow is finally, Christmas Day,
So it's early to bed, so we are out of the way,
First we leave some cake, for when Santa comes,
Mam says he'd also like a nice glass of rum.

THE MERMAID'S DANCE

As I walked along the ocean's shore,
I watched something amazing, I'd never seen before,
The ocean's waves met the cotton wool mist,
Caressed for a moment, then gently kissed
Taken back in surprise, I caught a glance,
Of beautiful mermaids, in synchronised dance,
They came from the mist, and a dance I saw,
Such precision like never before,
Surrounded by mist, they waved goodbye,
So taken back, I began to cry,
I was told a story, now I believe it's true,
That mermaids they dance, in memory of one crew,
Who lost their lives, and were never found,
Left lying, under the sea's sandy grounds,
The lady who told me, she says she's at ease,
As her man's in his heaven, under the great seas,
For each crew member, a mermaid was born,
In respect they dance, on a misty morn.

WHY DO THE LIVING SUFFER?

As time passes by, and hearts are broken,
People ask why? But no answer is spoken,
Babies for no reason, suddenly die,
Heartbroken parents, want to know why,
Children lose dads, or their mums,
Parents lose daughters, also their sons,
It's a question I often ask,
How does one cope, with such a task?
No-one can say, if the dead really feel,
But why for the living, don't the scars ever heal?
Living with pain, till it's their turn to die,
Remembering loved ones, they sit and cry,
You give us love, then we are forced to let go,
Is there a God? That's what I'd like to know.

IN THE TIME OF THE NINETIES

Today the world is full of disaster,
Crimes on the increase, poverty grows faster,
Lots of youngsters turned into thugs,
To feed their addiction, they have for drugs.

People are murdered, for no reason at all,
For grieving relatives, no explanation at all,
Their loved one's life has been stolen away,
That's what's going on in the world today.

Crime, rape, AIDS victims too,
How much more, can people go through,
God if you are there, answer me please,
When will all the bad things ever cease?

KENNETH MOOD

Born in Gateshead, Tyne and Wear. BA Hons Degree in Art and Design at Sunderland. At college I began to write poems, plays and songs.. Words were used in my etchings, drawings and paintings. I write about spiritual things, nature in towns and countryside. I get my ideas from all over the place, things I do, things I see, things I hear, using all my senses to create images of feelings. My religious poems are important to me because they make me understand my relationship with God. My other poems are a different perspective, showing areas of life which are interesting. I also paint and draw, enjoy gardening and songwriting, things seem to help each other, add to my creativity and knowledge of the world.

I like all types of poetry, often working on different themes, so I can build a big canvas, showing different areas, which gives more depth, using the element of surprise and fun. Some poems seem to write themselves, they come out of the blue and I've got to write them down. I collect odd verses and expand different lines, each poem seems to lead to the next, I always have different projects going on at the same time. I have God's gift.

I am also involved in film extra work, I've been in many productions; Catherine Cookson's films, *Tide of Life, The Gambling Man, Heartbeat, Peak Practice, Crocodile Shoes II, Spender, Ivanhoe, Byker Grove* and many more, over the years.

LIVING FOR THE LORD

It's easy living for the Lord,
It's easy doing His Will,
Like a child, I play on this earth,
Not worrying about material things.

If I go my wicked ways,
I will be dead,
Half a man, half a God.
Just think how foolish man can be,
To waste his time, looking for treasure,
While all the time, his heart is his key
To success.
The birds and bees do not worry,
So I live with God in perfect harmony.

WE LOVE YOU LORD

When the Lord speaks to you,
Please listen, for He is your Leader,
And wanting to forgive your sins,
Nobody is perfect we all have faults,
So listen, and wait for His guidance.

How many times have we done things
Wrong and felt guilty about the situation.
If only we had listened to the Lord, He knows
Our heart; the bad things in our life can be
Changed and we can live in the light, being
Filled with the Holy Spirit. Open the door
Of your heart and let Jesus in.

BATTLE-CRY

Fighting battles in the dark, can be a lonely business.
Always in a tangle in dark scenes,
It's the place the Devil likes best, putting us in shadows
And caves.

Feeling strong, after the battle, rising above all earthly
Dreams. Clear skies rescue me, so I can sail with the stars
And aeroplanes.

Decisions are different in a crisis,
Falling on barren ground, no growth, no energy, angry cries
From the crowd.
Thinking the road is clear and full of freedom.

Fighting battles I cannot win;
My faith protects me, when the storm is raging.
Love carries me to safe shores,
Where I hold on to my imagination and God.

CARRY ON

So afraid of the world,
Which leads me astray,
So afraid of the flesh,
Which leads me into temptation,
So afraid of the devil,
he fills me with corruption.

Thank God for my salvation,
Thank God for family and friends,
Thank God for the Holy Spirit,
Which makes me ten times stronger,
And gives me the will to carry on
Into God's glorious Kingdom.

MY SPIRITUAL HOME

Inside the church I see Jesus,
Showing me Heavenly things,
Angels stretch their wings,
Glowing, holding fruit and Kings.

As I pray, I feel calm, as if
Sitting on a beach watching
The seagulls glide across the sun.
As I pray, something is happening,
There is a ring of truth and comfort.

Inside the church, I feel as if I am home
Sitting in a ray of sunshine.
Laughing at the world, my dreams come alive,
My vision is bright, my future is safe
In God's hands tonight.

POWER OF THE LORD IN ACTION

People were saved at the front of the church,
The atmosphere was electric, people fell to
The floor, voices cried out for forgiveness,
Music lifted our hearts.
People bought tapes and books.

The preacher healed the sick.
We prayed for each other, there was hope
And glory, Jesus filled us with peace.
God was busy, people were saved,
And I was a witness.

YES LORD

Your voice is tender full of life, and truth,
As we walk together in another year, yet you
Are ahead of me,

There is still a love which glows far deeper
Than anything I've ever known,
Only you can give me contentment.

MY SAVIOUR

Shape me, love me like a Heavenly Father
Who cares,
Because here on earth, I have no heroes
But you.

And when I am changed, let me hear
Your voice, and feel the Holy Spirit
Flow inside my heart.

JESUS ON THE CROSS

My faith is growing,
Like the daffodils of Spring,
Like Wordsworth, I enjoy the love
Of nature; each time I pray,
I hope,
My family and friends,
Will share my faith.

ARE YOU GOING TO HEAVEN?

It's God's way, isn't it.
Death comes to us all,
As we sail away in Heaven,
The survivors bow their heads
And wonder, who is next.

It's God's way, who stays
And who goes first.
Passing through this life, entering
Another for eternity.
Everyone wonders if they'll see
Loved ones, showing love and kindness.

Yes, it's God's way,
Sweeping across the land,
Giving birth and death to families,
In all seasons, the promise of God's
Almighty hand.

CHURCHES UNITED

Churches came together, one Sunday night,
We prayed for one parent families,
Peace in Ireland and Iraq,
Preachers had vision, to fill St James' Park.
We came out the dark, and into the light.
We broke our negative thoughts,
Held hands and praised the Lord.

The money raised will help the homeless
And young people. The worship band celebrated
Victory. Preachers promised a new beginning.
I could feel something happening,
Churches together, encouraging, caring
And sharing. Praise the Lord, for such evenings.

RESTLESS SLEEP

Sometimes, I pray during the night,
Sometimes, I don't pray at all.
I often wonder if I should run away
And not be here at all.
But other days, I feel strong like ten horses
Or ten giants. That's when I feel the glory of
God in my bones.

Of course, when I'm low, feeling nothing is going
Right, I'm deep down in the mud with noisy
Monkeys, that's when I can't sleep, only moan
And groan.

Of course, when I pray, I'm rescued by the Lord,
Then I can play and run with moon and sun.
Talk with children and have picnics beside
The house where I was born, that's when I feel
Best, living in the light, not worrying about
Day or night.

DON'T BE DISCOURAGED

Don't be discouraged, look into your heart,
Feel the security, the warmth, the love of
The universe, forever overflowing, doing
God's business in you.

So sit back and enjoy the ride of a lifetime,
The Lord is the Leader, hold onto the horses,
And live in reality.
See the Holy place shining with glory,
Don't be discouraged, look into your God's eyes.

THIS IS THE BEST DAY OF MY LIFE

I'm not going to be angry today,
I'm going to love everybody I meet,
I will not let people burst my bubble,
Or moan or groan about the violence in
The street.
No, I say no, to negative thoughts, I shall
Walk with Jesus today,
Listen to His Word preach the Gospel,
In every situation, fill my mind and body
With spiritual things.

And in the evening I will set my table
With all the good things I have done,
And light a candle for peace and freedom.
And pray for the homeless and the pensioners,
Then send a cheque to Oxfam, and write a letter
To the Prime Minister, saying there should be
More love in the world and churches should
Be more united.

BE ALIVE

So many people drag you down into depression.
It's difficult to climb out of the pit.
What is the answer?
Listen to the Lord's voice,
He will provide ladders to get you out,
Be patient and obedient.

There is no easy road,
Life is full of sacrifice,
Watching our children grow, remember
The Father always wants the best for His children.

GOD LOVES A WINNER

Save me from boring days,
Save me from all my mistakes,
I want to live in perfect harmony,
And ride on a crest of a wave, with Jesus;
Working miracles, in every town,
Saving people from going down to the depths
Of despair.

Save me from miserable days,
Save me from a stony heart,
I want to run like the wind over valleys
Of green, looking at wild flowers which
Are rare, and breathe lots of country air.
I don't think I was made to be sad,
I don't think I was made to go mad,
I was made for spiritual reasons,
And day by day, God is showing me, it is so,
Beautiful being alive.

LOVE A STRANGER

Yes I have done wrong, I have walked in darkness.
My temptation has been strong, but now I know
Where I have gone wrong.

My light is shining for you Lord,
My heart is on fire with the word of goodness.
No more hurting words, only love shining through.

I lift my hands to the Lord,
And dance and sing.
He is the best God
With all the best players on His side, so how can
I fail, now I sing in the rain.

WHO IS IN CONTROL?

I try to do the best for my children,
But as usual I fail.
It's God who is winning, making them grow,
Like golden flowers.
Each hour, I wait on my chair, combing my
Thick brown hair.
My eyes gaze on their charm.
It's amazing how they farm their ideas to me.

Each morning is a miracle, overflowing joy my
Children show, turning on radios putting on
Shoes. I just sit being amazed, sitting in the
Shade in the kitchen, listening to radio four.

Then off they go to school, into a world of
Computers, trying to stay alive, and trying
To survive in a sea of homework.
Knowing, God is holding their hands, I can relax
And enjoy my marmalade and tea.

LOVE AND WISDOM

I'm lonely without the Lord.
Life is pointless,
Where has He gone,
Have I shut the door on Him?
I must pray and bring Him back.
My communication with wisdom
Is broken.
How can I survive without Him?

Each day is long,
Time is dragging on,
Why did I turn my back on the Lord?
I am the fool, so I repent my sins
And ask for forgiveness.
Please Lord let me win again,
Let me live life to the full,
Let me grow in Your love and wisdom.

WHY CAN'T I SEE?

When I've got a headache,
I blame the world,
When I'm old,
I blame the Devil,
When I'm sad,
I blame the rain.
It's stupid, feeling like this,
All my potential not being used,
Locked away for another day.
Rising above my feelings, I see great rivers of truth,
Washing over me, making me feel, born again, making me
Feel like Spring, full of hope and vision.

If only I felt like that all the time.
I know, where I'm going wrong, not listening to the Lord.
Somehow, I've tuned into a different channel,
And I always blame the weather or the people in the world,
Instead of myself.

BRIAN WILLIS (65)

Born and raised in Bolton, educated at Farnworth Grammar School and Royal Military Academy, Sandhurst. Commissioned in 1952, served in Germany, Nigeria, Thailand. I retired on medical grounds as major in 1969. Started to write verse as a pastime (along with lyric writing) while in the Forces.

After 3 years in consultancy, started working as Chamber of Commerce Executive in Bolton (1973), moving Coventry and Warwickshire Chamber in 1977.

I was asked (due to formation of Rhyme Revival) to write verse for 40th anniversary of bombing of Coventry Cathedral.

Dirk Bogarde agreed to record three sonnets for 'A' side of disc. He reluctantly agreed that there was a need for a 'B' side - hence the 'MP' sonnets. Regrettably the recordings were not well handled technically. Even worse, the production of the disc omitted 'responses' to the 'litany of reconciliation' and also left out the titles of the individual sonnets.

I am married to Elsie - have 2 adult children (one of each) and play golf, a game at which, despite practise, I find I can barely improve as I try to get better!

FOURTH REICH

High in the womb of the unknowing maid
snuggles the soldier of a score years hence.
Round her the while the battle-cry is made
'Come, Politician, sit upon this fence.'

Boredom is all we give the boys to eat,
Round us we scatter fertile seeds of doom
hoping our harvest will be one of wheat;
Knowing that someone has to reap the broom.

How long, how long can this be let to run?
Who has to face the folly of our day?
Will not the first to fall be someone's son?
When will the voice of reason have its say?

Somewhere a second Adolph seeks a place -
Find him a job - and save the human race!

MEMORY LANE

Your thoughts - those scenes that linger in the mind -
they pass with you, a loss to humankind.
Unless, that is, you freeze them in the frame
(transpose to word or film your Mem'ry Lane).
And when you read with love what you create
or rosily view the photographic vision,
they only say 'I'd better leave . . . I'm late!'
or welcome 'all these snapshots!' with derision.
You must not let the artiste in you down
nor must you *ever* pander to the base.
Whose conscience *can* you tote around the town?
To hide one's light is surely a disgrace!
If you were me, you'd write a verse or two
I'd tear the damned things up . . . if I were you!

NIGERIA - FREEDOM AT ANY PRICE?

When hackneyed pattern found Nigeria *free*
and chalk and cheese were married into dust;
when Logic cried 'Divide us into three!'
and high-grade crude was lava in the crust -
who could the honest peasant seek to trust?
Had not the *Bombaturi* gone away,
sickened to see his children's freedom day?

The newborn sallied wantonly to war,
supportive of another of her kind;
uncertain as to what the fight was for,
unless perhaps, with destiny in mind
she used her own myopia as a blind.
Thus she prepared to slash the price of blood,
damning her own arterial to the flood

that was to follow. As the gods perused
their several sons, they must have seen the way
in which their own divisive creeds had used
unprecedented innocence for sway -
presaging the disorder of today.
Could they discern which faults were ours or theirs?
Did mat or pew lend context to the prayers?

The song of Allah sung so long before
across and down the Harmattans of sand
had filtered through the Hausa-spoken lore
and given steel to custom that had stood
firm against the Victorian parenthood.
Pleased to be led - ecstatic when in charge -
the Northerners embraced the British Raj.

South, where the Guinea Current's fetid breath
greeted the Arab slavers with its plague;
west of the Niger's slimy, toothy death,
some of the Moslem forebears would renege
their role - to lie, to sleep, to love - and vague
is the bloodline lingering there today.
Although they turn to Mecca as they pray.

Locked like medieval virgins in a tower,
east of the Niger, walled by Cameroon;
known once as Ibos - (Biafrans in their hour);
this slavers' prey, though hostage to the moon
were quick to learn. Starved of tradition's boon
they swallowed all the pearls of Christianity,
wearing the strings to flatter British vanity.

Colonial Armies offered small variety,
reflecting more or less a British corps;
A lying microcosm of the society
they portrayed; Sandhurst training to the fore.
The frailest of Nations were all the more
protected by this front. Thus in the dance
of death, it first played shield - and then played lance!

The quality of leadership was fine,
extending to the tribal scholars; who
acclimatised as officers of the line,
where comradeship became a social glue
for most of them had been to Sandhurst too -
a place where, under international stress
it was not hard to feel togetherness.

The sergeants earned their corn by dint of sweat;
offering love and honour to the cause;
salt of the earth and highly trained - and yet
needing the constant prod of Army laws,
brooking reminders after every pause
in their ordered routine. Moreso their charge -
the soldiers, for whom discipline loomed large.

This then the shield - Nigeria's defense -
one force - one team - a credit to the land,
of friction unaware - and in a sense
one of the bases upon which we planned
to give her *freedom*. Fate then played its hand;
adding to all the factors in the plot
one single force. *Oil* was to be their lot.

Not in the North - where logistic blight
could have been balanced by the cultural base -
nor in the West with Lagos port in sight
but in the East where leaders chose to race
madly for *freedom* and away from grace.
'What's ours is mine' became the 'Christian' creed;
Freedom begat a litany of *greed*.

No civil war is ever really lost,
for winning hauls embarrassment in tow;
but Armies split by treason are a cost
more burdensome than most of us could know; -
a shield turns quickly to a lance - and so
the source of the stability of years
leads in a trice to strong men shedding tears.

Many were shed on England's leading pages -
'Pity the poor Biafran' was the cry;
nothing but passing time such bias assuages;
nothing but passing time deludes the lie,
allowing the pretence that eagles fly;
allowing us to see that Christianity
permits nor black nor white religious vanity.

And there is no way back from the abyss;
Strength may allow forgiveness - never trust!
God may reject the awfulness of this -
Allah will never reconvene the dust.
Apostles of Allah told us that *we must
not give the freedom others were demanding!*
We understood! - but were too 'understanding'

THE WESTMINSTER TRILOGY:
THE GREEN MP

I made my maiden speech the other day
spoke like a maiden, too, upon my soul!
I'll set the country right - in my own way
once I determine what's to be my role.

I'll influence, but will not be deflected
and I'll persuade or bully, yes indeed.
Was it to serve that I became elected?
Then will I serve when I observe the need!

I hear they're voting now upon defence -
is that a subject I feel strongly on?
Well, yes and no - resorting to pretence
could be the tactic to depend upon.

Just for the moment - vote the party way -
why should I stretch my soul - until my day?

THE BLUE MP

Now is my soul well stretched from meeting needs;
needs of the Party rather than of mine:
one of the flowers on which the Party feeds
for Parties feed on personal decline.

I should have struck when I was still in bud,
done me a Winston while I yet was green,
Oh I am sick and tired of being good,
something about the lobby is obscene!

Still there is time for me to hit the heaven,
the bench in front is not too far away.
Didn't she smile at me tonight at seven?
Didn't she sack a Minister today?

Couldn't there still be profit if I please her?
Couldn't my small ambition make me Caesar?

THE PURPLE MP

Now I have come to terms with what is mine
Mine is the lot of many a reserve.
So very slender the dividing-line
which favours those who get what none deserve.

O, I have been as often man as mouse;
taken for granted, yes, but taken whole.
Full man enough to reach the Upper House,
where I now wrestle with my new-found soul.

Gone are the 'us' and 'them' of yesteryear,
here is the inner-conscience given rein
causing the pit-face Tory to appear,
uttering words which used to cause *him* pain.

Here as a mellow fellow I shall stay;
forgetting the cause - remembering the fray.

1970 IN THE UNION . . .
THE LEADER

I won my spurs a mere decade ago,
through being over-zealous, truth to tell.
I never learned the fourteen phrases, although
Arthur Scargill says I'm doing well!
There is no confrontation I would shirk;
each problem, large or small I'll treat alike.
One thing outweighs entitlement to work -
a democratic right to go on strike!
Unanimous, we seek our even star.
Why should a brother live on charity?
Each nurse, each farm-hand shall afford a car,
through free collective bargaining - and parity!
Equality in all things is essential,
so shall it be . . . upon my differential!

THE MEMBER

How do I view this fellow that I follow,
this brother that I cannot call a friend?
At times I see his claims as vague and hollow -
at others he makes statements I'd defend.
What is the basis of our joint position,
is it a product of our history?
How did he get there - was it my decision?
Is his kind sponsored by the likes of me?
Was he, I wonder, master of our trade
too good to stay o'er long at his machine
or was he somehow - as it were - mislaid
only to rise much later on the scene?
Now in this dawning age of worker bosses,
would we make gains, with him in charge . . . or losses!

THE COVENTRY SONNETS:
ST MICHAEL'S CATHEDRAL 1373-1940

Your beauty took six hundred years to mould
And but one-hundred minutes to excise,
As firemen with an empty hose to hold
Could only watch you burn before their eyes.

Bright spirit - you are still within that spire,
And must have seen the cindering of your frame,
For sure you helped the phoenix from the fire
And still found time to love the foe who came

To torture you! The love that you impart
Appeals to all the good there is in Man
It nurtures the compassion in his heart
As no degree of human pleading can;

For tho' he kneels at newer altar-rails
He finds forgiveness at your Cross of Nails.

THE COVENTRY SONNETS:
COVENTRY CATHEDRAL

Proudly she stands at stricken Michael's side -
Church of the world, to which the world belongs.
Keeping her flock forever open-eyed
As she ignores the carping critics' tongues.

O you, the few, the screaming pale minority;
You who would have us re-create St Paul -
Time to away, and 'cede to the majority,
Those who can feel the wonder of it all!

Hewn from the awful power of modern love,
Built to erase a thousand years of hate,
Destined to show that man can rise above
The dismal doings of his Father's fate.

Here, where the Devil struck without impunity
Stands this new testament to global unity.

BEGINNING

Speaking of love, that all-abiding pain
which pays the bearer nothing but despair -
I say the words whose saying keeps me sane
but lack the soul to lay my conscience bare.

Talking of love? I do that rather well
and talking takes the heat out of my fire
but fails to warm a heart that suffers hell
and leaves the preacher feeling like a liar.

Being in love is but to love alone;
offering what you cannot give or take.
Loving is fine - but when the loving's done
love is no longer something you can make.

Lovers are those who have partaken of
my dream. I haven't. I am just in love.

EGO

I often wish that God would take advice.
With my small star ascending He could learn
so much from me - of life - its gifts, its price -
and I would seek so little in return.

I know He sees the flaws in others' thought
as easily as I; and with His power
to lead the hearts and minds of man, He ought
to take advantage of my measured hour.

Thus could He have His way without the strain
that must exist when lesser mortals ride
life's chariot; let Him hand me the rein
and I will offer heaven back its pride.

This is the destiny He must afford -
for have I not agreed to call Him Lord?

CHRISTINA M CLARKE

I am 54 years of age and was born in Birmingham in 1944. I have lived in Cirencester, Gloucestershire for 12 years. I have two sons and two lovely grandsons. I became a mature student in my late 30's studying English language, English literature and Sociology. I have enjoyed writing poetry from my early teens but over the last ten years I have seen my work more seriously as an emotional and thought-provoking process. Inspiration for my poetry comes from my own personal experiences, feelings and observations on life. I have had numerous poems published in various anthologies and I am a distinguished member of the International Society of Poets, and have been awarded two certificates of merit.

I am profoundly affected by the world and suffering, its sadness and its cruelty. I am therefore compelled to write about material issues and emotions, but I have been blessed with a wicked sense of humour and fortunately can see the funny side of most things in life. This is reflected in my poetry writing, a humorous slant on life as I see it. I also very much enjoy writing poems for children and it is an ambition of mine that one day I will publish a children's book of poetry.

Up until March of 1997 when I was unfortunate to be involved in an accident, I was an enthusiastic charity worker for my local Oxfam shop, and was a keen member of the Cirencester Operatic Society. (I love the theatre and swimming, seeing friends and family, needlepoint and not forgetting my much-loved mad moggie, Suki, who is the inspiration for my cat poetry).

PORTRAITS

A happy face -
A worried frown
A party dress -
A wedding gown.
On my wall framed with care
All my family hanging there.

Children and teddy bears,
A Grandmother who cares.
In quiet spectator fashion they -
Look down whilst in my bed I lay.
My comfort as I fall asleep,
Family vigil through the night will keep.
And as I wake I can hear them say -
Welcome to another day.

AND BEYOND IS THE SEA

Warm mellow walls grey-tiled roofs,
Tiny chintzed windows that's for me,
And beyond is the sea.

Bright blue skies, seagulls cry overhead,
Palms growing wild midst geraniums that's for me,
And beyond is the sea.

Quaint inns and shops, air fresh tinged with salt,
Boisterous winds, old world charm that's for me,
And beyond is the sea.

Picture postcard scenery from my window to view,
One day I hope this is what I'll come home to;
When I grow old - that's for me -
And beyond is the sea . . .

THE TRIP

Nanna I'm so tired I can hardly keep awake.
But I know we're nearly there and it's going to be such fun,
But Nanna, it seems a long long way -
And it's hot here in the sun.

I've got my bucket and spade and my sandwiches as well,
I'm terribly excited, Nanna can't you tell?
You've pointed out the scenery and we've eaten all the sweets,
We've played a game you called 'Eye Spy'. but you promised
other treats.

Listen Nanna - the engine makes a soothing sound
And it's jogging us along,
But I'm feeling rather sleepy, please Nanna sing a song.
Oh! Nanna it really seems a long long way -
We've been travelling nearly all the day.

This sitting still is very hard when I long to run about,
I want to run along the beach, throw my ball and shout.
But Nanna, I'll just have a little nap, please may I climb onto your lap?
Nanna are we nearly there? It's so hot here in the sun,
But I do know Nanna that when we are it's going to be such fun.

THE BEGINNING

On first meeting
        That unfathomable spark -
Lit up the space between us.
        Where nothing had been before
Came an understanding -
        Called friendship between two people . . .

AUTUMN PUSSY CAT

There is a pussy cat out there,
Who doesn't have time to sit and stare.
He's watching the autumn leaves
Floating in the air.

A long striped body from nose to tail,
Pussy leaps to no avail.
When he jumps he must be quick,
To catch them out is the trick.

Red and yellow and gold and brown,
Lie all the leaves on the ground.
Nice and crunchy under paws,
This is much more fun than playing indoors.

Perhaps if puss jumped up the tree,
As close as close as he could be,
He'd catch the leaves before they fall,
And be back down in no time at all.

Dear little puss didn't you know,
Autumn leaves always fall before winter's snow.
And all the trees will soon be bare,
So puss will have to find something else to do -
Until autumn comes again next year . . .

TREASURED TIME

Life is so precious don't you know
We just take it for granted, until -
Life takes a turn, a dramatic event
It brings us up short, sometimes heaven-sent.

A reminder as we are rushing about
Doing ten things at once, all important no doubt,
That nothing is worth more than life itself
And of sharing with loved ones lots more of yourself.

Taking time to laugh, to wonder love and live,
To show our emotions, to receive and to give.
To nurture the bonds that bind us all to -
This Earth created for me and for you.

So treasure the time as it slips quickly by,
There's so much to enjoy if we only try.
Life's pleasures I know for some are so few,
So stop - lift your face to the sun - take a deep breath
                                    And start life anew . . .

FOR THE LOVE OF A CAT

Stare if you will my enigmatic cat
Eyes green pools of depthless liquid -
They seek to pierce my very soul perhaps.
Under your gaze I guiltily blink -
And turn away from your stare
Lest you see the secrets within.

I know you can bend me against my will,
Make me serve you when I would rather be still.
Oh! Gracious cat, I am just a human being,
I haven't your gifted powers, your extra-sensory all-seeing.
I will do whatever you bid me do, I will read it in your stare,
I am only here to serve your every need - but cat -
I know there are some things with me you deign to share.

I am humble when you stroke my cheek,
Grateful for that touch that we both seek,
Because you know just when to comfort me -
With your gentle touch,
That's why I have to thank you and say I love you very much . . .

GOODWILL TO ALL MEN

In the depths of winter's chill
I hear the blackbird loud and shrill,
Proclaiming Christmas is very near
For some a joy, for others a tear.

Warmly wrapped children play in the snow
Laughter and fun despite wind winter's blow.
A few children huddle, no gloves or scarves for them,
Isn't Christmas wonderful? Goodwill to all men.

Hurry along, soon be home in the warm,
There's the trimmings to do and tree to adorn;
Christmas cake to make and mince pies too -
Why are these young people huddled together
On this cold winter's morn - haven't they
Anything better to do?

Moving closer I see the rags on their backs,
White faces frozen under those old sacks.
The snow is falling harder now and will
Soon be very deep -
People are walking faster, snow crunching under feet.

Brightly coloured packages, fir trees tucked -
Tightly under arms,
Families warm and snug indoors,
They're never going to come to harm.
But for faces that disappear beneath our feet;
No chance of just one Christmas treat.
No glowing faces and warm homes for them,
Isn't Christmas wonderful? Goodwill to all men.

VISIONS OF THE FUTURE

Visions of the future and the fear that lies within,
Memories of freedom and laughter where did it all end.
I look upon the children their tiny faces bright,
our heritage, their future, I cannot see the light.

Uncertainty and terror are watchwords now,
No more alone we seek a quiet place -
To ease the worried brow.
forced to be herded, protection uppermost,
Lawlessness, murder and rape beset us coast to coast.

Visions of the future my heart breaks as I mourn,
For passing days of freedom sweet and future -
Childhood of newborn.
Innocence is now no more, wise beyond their years,
The glimmerings of hope fading through the tears.
Children old and worn, breathing poison with every breath -
Around every corner we come face to face with death.

Look down across the meadows, golden in the sun,
And smell the smell of sweet, sweet grass the animals graze on.
The sky so blue, the clouds so white -
How much longer I wonder will we see this sight.
Visions of the future, it could all be wonderful again -
Beauty, purity and harmony -
If man's conscience and truth be our future aim . . .

THE LITTLE CHRISTMAS TREE

How sad the little Christmas tree lying in the dark,
All year forgotten in some attic corner with last year's
tinsel and peeling plastic bark.
'Once' said the little Christmas tree talking to itself -
'I sat in wondrous splendour upon a large oak shelf.'
'How wonderful it was,' the little tree did sigh,
'All the glitter and presents from there I did espy.
Lovely candles I held aloft and a star upon my head,
And lights and baubles on my branches were bedecked.
The children laughed and danced around and worshipped
Me I know, and from my perch I could see myself -
Reflected in the window.'
The little tree sadly sighed as it recalled the happy scene,
Then a glittery tinsel tear broke the happy dream.
'It seemed very long ago' thought the little tree.
'I wonder if anyone will still remember me, and take me
From this dreary place -
So I can once again see the children with smiles upon
Their face.'
The little tree did slumber on in the cold and dark,
When suddenly a voice was heard, the children had
Returned, and thought it such a lark -
To pluck the little Christmas tree from its resting place,
And with joyous laughter into the house did race.
The little tree did quiver with such delight,
As once more with branches decorated and bright
It stood again upon the shelf the object of great joy.
The little tree smiled knowing that once, just for a little
While, life would be that happy dream and its
Purpose would fulfil -
In making children wonder at this sight so magical.
'Oh thank you, thank you' said the little tree
Standing proud and tall -
'For allowing me to make this Christmas the happiest
of all. . .'

THE FLAME OF LIFE

The flame of life is burning in every heart tonight.
Give us the courage to keep it burning bright.
Hope that faith and wisdom too -
In all our endeavours will justly see us through.

Give us the strength in tooth and nail,
To withstand our foes as we assail,
Though there are obstructions all around,
And difficulties abound.

Let our spirit carry us, give us strength to overcome.
Let our errors be our learning, forgive all, not just some.
Keep determination in every mighty breast.
However long the journey, do not give up the quest . . .

THE TOAST

Here's to fate, to new horizons,
Not knowing the future and what life has in store.
Here's to friends' lives intertwined together,
For what purpose we can never be sure.

Here's to past lives and those to come.
Here's to our dreams, life's mysteries and more.
Here's to families wherever they are,
And our decisions right or wrong -
To our contributions on the stage of life,
Awaiting that encore.

Here's to beloved ones those present and those gone,
Maybe we'll meet again someday,
Meanwhile here's to health and happiness -
And all our futures to come . . .

BABY SLEEP ON

Sleep on my baby sleep on,
Your soft cheek flushed like a rosebud.
A tiny hand resting on my breast
I will not disturb your rest.

Breathe deep my baby, breathe deep,
Warm breath on my face as you sleep,
Little knees tucked up like a kitty cat.
As you dream your curling lashes
Flutter velvet black.

Dream on baby, dream on,
Stir not till slumber's at an end,
Time standing still
As sleep's mountain peak you ascend.

Awaken gently baby, awaken gently,
Open your eyes and you will see -
Your safe and warm to my bosom clasped,
The time you slept was but a moment passed.

SHADOWS IN THE FIRE

Flickering firelight,
A magic lantern show,
In ever-changing scenes
I conjure up imaginary foe.

The ever-changing scenes,
Flickering firelight.
Faces glowing hot and pink -
As I search for meaning in those coals so bright.

A land of never, never -
Over smoking hills aglow,
The images, forgotten faces -
As I drift and wonder I see ashes turn to snow.

In ever-changing scenes -
Dark shadows of the never come to life
A magic lantern show
Flickering firelight . . .

LOTUS BLOSSOM MAIDENS

Three maids with parasols on high,
Collecting lotus blossom petals as they
                                float by . . .
Embroidered kimonos dazzle in the sun,
Flower bedecked heads - maidens ordinary
                                to some . . .

But not I, for as these maids swish their silky robes,
And peep coyly from under parasols,
Like butterflies they flit and flutter, alighting here
                                and there . . .
Softly laughing, I cannot help but gaze at rays -
Glinting on coal-black tresses of their hair.

There they stand in daylight bright,
Their heads aglow, a halo of white.
It seems unreal this unselfconscious scene,
Ever elusive like a passing dream.

Oh! The perfection of this delightful sight,
I can never say that I have not seen aught
This sight is precious by far and more,
Than any pleasure bought . . .

JAMES HODGSON

I was born in Leeds, an only child brought up with the boy next door who was bigger and older than I was

My parents were both keen on sports, as was the boy next door, and my early childhood was spent playing games at which I was woefully inadequate. So, Father devised a regime which would ensure I did not grow up to be a sissy. This consisted of ice-cold baths every morning and a brisk rub-down with a rough towel and, on the day of rest, continuous competitive games.

I finally escaped being sent away to school where a percipient master introduced me to English Literature which I studied for many happy hours producing a treatise on Shakespeare and Shaw.

Having failed my matriculation exam, Father asked me how I intended to make a living and, when I replied by writing plays, he sent me to the nearest School of Architecture.

Meanwhile I had written a children's play about 'The Emperor's New Clothes' which was produced by the Leeds Arts Theatre. However, my dramatic career was interrupted by the war.

Demobilised six years later I finished my course at the Architectural College and obtained employment in a Birmingham practice. This enabled me to visit Stratford where I saw the RSC in every play by Shakespeare except Titus Andronicus.

Eventually joining a partnership in Dewsbury I spent the rest of my working life designing carbuncles and writing verse.

Alone in my retirement I am grateful for the gifts of memory and imagination which is the world in which I now live.

MACBETH

How my dagger finger itches
to be rid of those three witches
for the way that they betrayed my well laid plots

And of Banquo that wet blanket
who upset our royal banquet
playing ghost before mine host who got the trots

As for motherless Macduff
I have had more than enough
of his whinging and his whining Wyandottes

Yet more threatening than this is
my somnambulating Mrs
with her latest spate of superating spots

For as Birnam wood creeps nearer
and the yellow leaves grow searer
will I still be top of bill as King of Scots?

THE TEMPEST

Now our revels all are ended
least is said is soonest mended
God forgive us those offended

Every goose has got her gander
Caliban his island and a
Ferdinand admired Miranda

No more clowns with funny noses
gone the days of wine and roses
finally the curtain closes.

HAMLET

I am sitting on the loo
undecided what to do
and thinking on the king my father's death

and upon my mother too
and carbuncled uncle who
is steeped in gore more deeply than Macbeth

and I have not got a clue
if the old mole told me true
poor ghost alas my only shibboleth

So Horatio adieu
Now the rest is up to you
and silence I am running out of breath

ROMEO AND JULIET
Prologue
Enter Chorus

Two houses back to back one up and down
in old Verona where this play begins
whose doleful tenants terrorise the town
with demarcation disputes no one wins
beget a brace of drug-addicted brats
who woo and wed in Godly father's cell
and so to bed to copy alley cats
indifferent to what their stars foretell
how he curtails her kinsman in the feud
and flees the city lest he lose his head
while she awakes in ghostly solitude
beside the bones of her ancestral dead
the which if you are interested stay
to see the four-day passage of our play.

TWELFTH NIGHT

How lovely to live in Illyria
a haven of memorabilia
it is nicer than Nice
not as greasy as Greece
And Cannes cannot compare
with its redolent air
from masses of bright bougainvillaea

How lovely to live in Illyria
with those with whom one is familiar
Uncle Toby et al
and his clodpole tall pal
Sir A Aguecheek
an inebriate freak
who waxes progressively sillier

How lovely to live in Illyria
obsessed with one's own juvenilia
where Malvolio knows
wearing cross-gartered hose
from the toes to the knee
is the best recipe
to tourniquet his haemophilia

How lovely to live in Illyria
except when the weather turns chillier
then the residents say
the rain rains every day
to augment the salt tears
of those two doleful dears
Duke Orsino and Lady Olivia

OTHELLO

Othello was a fellow
more sinned against than sinning
particularly mellow
provided he was winning

But when the honest Iago
let slip a little slander
the subsequent farrago
made green his black commander

who damning Desdemona
for playing hanky-panky
With Cassio Casanova
And hubby's mummy's hanky

to salve his wounded honour
condemned himself to death
and fell defunct upon her
which made her gasp for breath

Sing Willow willow willow
        she had a dunlopillo

RICHARD THE THIRD

I never killed our Clarence
as many people think
he simply lost his balance
and fell into the drink

About the late Lord Hastings
his ending I foresaw
enjoying lewd lambastings
laid on by Mistress Shore

A little hesitation
between me and my friend
cost Buckingham his station
and most untimely end

Undoubtedly the princes
parted from their mother
as history evinces
smothered one another

AS YOU LIKE IT

Avoid the Forest of Arden
        everyone wants to come here
where the thickets are quick
with Tom Harry and Dick
charging like Tennyson
after the venison
who flee through the Forest in fear

Abjure the Forest of Arden
        everyone wants to come here
where the Smiths and the Jones
carve their surnames on stones
and true love's devotees
their initials on trees
around which their canines career

Where is that Forest of Arden
        when nobody ever came here
then the woods were as green
as a sea-sick marine
and each hart sought each hind
with but one thought in mind
which was as you like it my dear

TITUS ANDRONICUS
(A Shakespearian Pot Boiler)

This is a horror story
of rapine rape and lust
two heads both crushed and gory
encased in pastry crust

concocted for their mother
who ravenously ate
the one after the other
unconscious of its fate

Her sons cut short by Titus
whose daughter they entrapped
then ravished to affright us
tongue-tied and handicapped

because her father slaughtered
their mother's eldest son
and hanged him drawn and quartered
for being born a Hun

She soon retaliated
by dealing death for death
his sons decapitated
without a pause for breath

At Titus's suggestion
replete with home-made pie
and chronic indigestion
she knew she was to die

He slew her single-handed
and then himself was slain
The party was disbanded
and those who did remain

were either dead or dying
sic transit vomitus
or not for want of trying
tight as Andronicus

THE TAMING OF THE SHREW

When a macho man
woos a froward shrew
this is what he can
and she cannot do

If he wants to wed
somewhat oddly dressed
he can go ahead
she cannot protest

When he cannot sleep
she must stay awake
busy counting sheep
for her husband's sake

Should he choose to fast
she too must comply
her austere repast
being humble pie

If you wish to know
how to tame a shrew
ask Petruchio
for a tip or two

THE MERCHANT OF VENICE
A tale of double-dealing

Big businessman Antonio
is feeling rather sad
because his beau Bassanio
belies his sugar dad
in spite of all the ready dough
he has already had

At home in Belmont Portia waits
Bassanio to wed
Her suitors learning of their fates
to abstinence are fled
In secrecy she contemplates
which words best rhyme with lead

As Shylock seals his merry bond
a pound of flesh in lieu
ensuring he will not be conned
for being born a Jew
his daughter hurries to abscond
and with a Gentile too

His argosies gone all astray
Antonio is broke
His creditor weighs up his prey
the debt he will invoke
for every dog must have his day
And Shylock does not joke

A Daniel to judgement cries
a voice within the court
as Portia enters in disguise
the usurer to thwart
deceiving him about his prize
and leaving him distraught

so artifice beats avarice
and Shylock is forsworn
At Belmont all is wedded bliss
upon this happy morn
as in a Venice ghetto is
a Christian reborn

ALL'S WELL
THAT ENDS WELL

Keen to join the upper classes
Helena is making passes
at her patroness's son

He the eldest of his farrow
recently head boy at Harrow
now the Count du Rousillon

who to dodge the maid's advances
at the double off to France is
with his mother's blessing gone

After him the doctor's daughter
with a cure her father taught her
to restore the King anon

who has promised she shall marry
any young Tom Dick or Harry
she has set her heart upon

If you think the tale well ended
than you have misapprehended
All is Well has just begun

ANTONY AND CLEOPATRA
Enobarbus speaks

She left him in the market place
hopping lightly on one foot
while Antony stared into space
up with which he could not put

The stool he sat on was too small
ever to withstand the weight
of he who holds a world in thrall
one of Rome's triumvirate

The square was empty but for air
none about to lend their ears
only posters everywhere
advertising souvenirs

The whole of Egypt was en fete
watching their bewitching queen
with rod and line herself as bait
fishing for her libertine

Cleopatra anaconda
wily serpent of old Nile
knowing absence makes one fonder
has good reason for her smile

ERIC ALLDAY

I was a member of the West Riding Constabulary seconded to the Foreign Office during the '39-'45 war and served as a staff officer with Military Government, later with the Special Police Corps in Germany. In 1949 I joined the Probation Service and retired as a senior officer in 1976.

Since then I have been engaged in voluntary work with the Adult Literacy Scheme, the local counselling service and, since its opening in 1983, with St Giles Hospice at Whittington near Lichfield.

When I retired I was determined to devote more time to study and reading. I had been deeply affected by the death of two sons and felt a compulsion to understand more about life and death.

After years of study, prayer and meditation I began to realise that not only was there a higher self but that it was possible to actually experience it, not merely to intellectualise it.

Having had several meaningful revelations, graciously given, my poetry began to be very much influenced by this enlightenment. I have had several poems published and a booklet produced in aid of the Hospice funds.

I am a widower and a member of the Churches' Fellowship for Psychical and Spiritual Studies, whose motto is 'To faith add knowledge'.

A past Chairman and now an honorary member of the City of Lichfield Probus Club. I am interested in art, writing and music and I play bowls and snooker regularly. For many years I was President of Photographic Societies in Lichfield and Stafford and am now an honorary member.

THE DREAMER DREAMS ME

The dreamer of the night
hovers round my mind
until the morning light
when dreams are left behind.

In sleep he is elusive
but never wanders far
in spite of my divisive
thoughts, often most bizarre.

In deepest slumber
far and wide he strays
but then the wonder
is He always with me stays.

Beyond the solid thought
which melts at close of day,
His vision's almost caught
but ever gets away.

Then suddenly a flash - no more,
and in a kind of trance
I sense a closing door,
but not before an entrance

in such a Virgin Light
of mysterious duality,
a wondrous delight,
a sign of immortality?

And so the dreamer
dreams me evermore
a most persistent schemer
whose love for me is sure.

FIVE HAIKU ÉTUDES

In silence beyond
the infinity of mind
Light creates insight.

Seek within the heart
heavenly love and power
present hour by hour.

Search the Higher Self
for the truth you have long sought
the Divine is there.

The supreme virtue
Love radiates from the soul
wants nothing itself.

Your love has not gone
says the voice of Silence
the soul still lives on.

THE PLANT SO RARE

Eliminate the noisy turmoil,
the feverish unceasing activity
of Western Man in his city,
far removed from the soil
from which seed-like he emerged;
remove his avaricious aim
from a soul so weak and lame
in materialistic search submerged;
preserve Oh Lord the care
now lost amongst the weeds,
smothered by sordid deeds;
spread the *love* that plant so rare.

THE COSMIC JOURNEY

Unseen threads weave
and intermingle:
countless atoms leave
not one single
planet immune,
nor any living thing,
all are there in tune
with the Cosmic Ring,
swirling through space
on journeys manifest,
bearing the human race
towards the highest crest,
where thoughts unite
and science proves
philosophy right,
and spirit moves
towards its final goal;
Mankind then will find
the *One* becomes the whole
and all is in the Mind.

BEYOND THE INTELLECT

Man's tiny limited mind
is unable to understand things
beyond his finite intellect,
such knowledge from faith in God springs;
experience leads to the deeper life,
The Divine in the commonplace brings
wisdom in spite of the intellect.

The Higher Self enlightenment reveals
in the form of intuition and insight,
this Inner Light, God's radiance within,
leads to that which is out of sight;
we can connect with this source
if we seek aright
and live from its authority
from our Inner Temple of Light,
healing the past creating the future.

DOUBTS

Adrift with deepest thought
in a sea of disbelief
losing what had long been sought;
the quickened grief
saps the power of will,
with each wave I seek
the haven which may still
a faith made weak
by the surging tide
of mass despair; I drift
to the distant side,
the current now so swift
carries me far beyond
all earthly doubts and fears
and I sense a bond
with the Power that hears,
which will safely guide
and light again the way
to a harbour deep inside.

TOUCH

Senses play upon the soul
in a good or evil way
enrich or destroy our divine role
as we live from day to day.

Sight sound smell taste
the greatest of all is touch
so often our gifts we waste
and lose the Godly crutch.

Touch is a heavenly gift
'sensory' experience profound
but we need to sense the rift
with 'sensual' not confound.

Touch relaxed and released
needed by all without exception,
life's sorrows thus decreased
strengthened our sense of perception.

Touch is felt emotionally
by a tug upon the soul,
moving us spiritually
to love and to console.

Touch activates other senses
to an unmistakable degree,
strengthens our defences
setting our minds free.

Touch imprints itself on everything
its name is pyschometry,
understanding of the self will bring
help in our search for symmetry.

Touch is a natural instinct
to calm or peace bestow,
quite clearly is distinct
from the mundane life's flow.

Touch an aspect of divinity,
Christ healed by its use,
symbolic of the Trinity,
conveying a heavenly truce.

Touch of hands a kiss on the lip
passionless but transfiguring,
with God denotes a kinship,
relief to the suffering will bring.

Touch then is the conductor of sensation,
from it smell taste music can arise,
self-healing and acts of creation
with lead man in time to paradise.

FLIGHT

Glorious the movement in our sight,
hawk and gull, swift and swallow,
their joyful play a pure delight.
Eager eyes must gladly follow
such wondrous graceful daring flight,
thrill with those symbolic swerves,
hail the aerial Aphrodite
controlling acrobatic curves,
a silhouette against the light,
form and movement in a wave,
dancing and swirling like a kite,
a final plunge, a last octave,
then gracefully the stars alight.

DEATH OF A BELOVED

There is a desolate
disorientation
piercing my inmost self,
not lamentation
not common grief;
surrounded by silence
devastatingly intense,
forcing my soul
into the abyss of suspense;
yet I am deeply aware
God does care,
in this dark night of despair
the dawn will still be there;
but oh, the loneliness, the stress
surging through my Being;
desperately I cling to my belief,
awaiting the new day
of compassionate relief,
knowing it will come,
knowing, though wearisome,
it will be heaven-sent.

SCIENTIFIC PHILOSOPHY

Quantum or Relativity
can both be true?
But for brevity,
for the very few
laymen who understand,
subject and object are one;
on the other hand
just for the fun
of it space and time
are changeable not fixed;
it's a wicked crime
Man has long been tricked;
it seems we can connect
interact and participate
but cannot without effect
observe - only dissipate;
things ain't what they seem
to be - what about ESP?
Is life just a dream?
Does one really see?
Did Newton point the way
or Einstein's insight
confirm Socrates' lay?

Or has God got it right?

THE HOSPICE

A hospice is not set apart
from Life itself, so do take heart
when entering this quiet place
'twill surely bring us face to face
with our true Self; now we may start

to find the peace which lies within,
now is the moment we'll begin
to sense the mystery of time
and feel a presence most sublime,
to lose all hope would be a sin;

Let not the bitterness which sours
steal the beauty from the flowers,
though body may be sick and worn
the Spirit lives to greet the dawn
and blesses our remaining hours.

OLD AGE

To be old is not necessarily to be wise,
Age is not synonymous with wisdom,
This we all must realise
in this Earthly Kingdom,
'There's no fool like an old fool'
is an adage too oft told;
Though passions may begin to cool,
and man's no longer bold,
yet something must remain
in this closing stage,
when love of life may wane
and against an ageing self comes rage;
Love itself holds the key
and does not fade with age,
Man does not cease to be
but prepares to turn another page.

THE PEARL OF ETERNITY

The ignorance of humanity
stems from habitual identification
with the body alone,
neglecting its inborn divinity,
its inward and eternal home;
the outer life is but a travesty
of our true immortal state

sadly seen as a commodity
competitively offered for sale,
a means of evaluating personality;
success depends on how we get it across,
life now is measured by an ability
to sell ourselves to the highest bidder.

Forsaken is our spirituality,
little attempt is made to find
the heavenly kingdom of infinity,
beyond all earthly time and space.

Why do we not seek this *pearl of eternity*
waiting there within ?
We must begin, begin, begin!